The relation betweene the lord of a mannor and the coppy-holder his tenant delivered in the learned readings of the late excellent and famous lawyer Char. Calthrope (1635)

Charles Calthrope

The relation betweene the lord of a mannor and the coppy-holder his tenant delivered in the learned readings of the late excellent and famous lawyer Char. Calthrope

Calthrope, Charles, Sir, d. 1616.
Signatures: [A] B-N4 O2.
Errata: p. [1] at end.
Imperfect: print show-through.
[2], 99, [1] p.
London : Printed for William Cooke, and are to be sold at his shop neere Furnivals Inne-gate in Holborne, 1635.
STC (2nd ed.) / 4369.5
English
Reproduction of the original in the Harvard University Library

Early English Books Online (EEBO) Editions

Imagine holding history in your hands.

Now you can. Digitally preserved and previously accessible only through libraries as Early English Books Online, this rare material is now available in single print editions. Thousands of books written between 1475 and 1700 and ranging from religion to astronomy, medicine to music, can be delivered to your doorstep in individual volumes of high-quality historical reproductions.

We have been compiling these historic treasures for more than 70 years. Long before such a thing as "digital" even existed, ProQuest founder Eugene Power began the noble task of preserving the British Museum's collection on microfilm. He then sought out other rare and endangered titles, providing unparalleled access to these works and collaborating with the world's top academic institutions to make them widely available for the first time. This project furthers that original vision.

These texts have now made the full journey -- from their original printing-press versions available only in rare-book rooms to online library access to new single volumes made possible by the partnership between artifact preservation and modern printing technology. A portion of the proceeds from every book sold supports the libraries and institutions that made this collection possible, and that still work to preserve these invaluable treasures passed down through time.

This is history, traveling through time since the dawn of printing to your own personal library.

Initial Proquest EEBO Print Editions collections include:

Early Literature

This comprehensive collection begins with the famous Elizabethan Era that saw such literary giants as Chaucer, Shakespeare and Marlowe, as well as the introduction of the sonnet. Traveling through Jacobean and Restoration literature, the highlight of this series is the Pollard and Redgrave 1475-1640 selection of the rarest works from the English Renaissance.

Early Documents of World History

This collection combines early English perspectives on world history with documentation of Parliament records, royal decrees and military documents that reveal the delicate balance of Church and State in early English government. For social historians, almanacs and calendars offer insight into daily life of common citizens. This exhaustively complete series presents a thorough picture of history through the English Civil War.

Historical Almanacs

Historically, almanacs served a variety of purposes from the more practical, such as planting and harvesting crops and plotting nautical routes, to predicting the future through the movements of the stars. This collection provides a wide range of consecutive years of "almanacks" and calendars that depict a vast array of everyday life as it was several hundred years ago.

Early History of Astronomy & Space

Humankind has studied the skies for centuries, seeking to find our place in the universe. Some of the most important discoveries in the field of astronomy were made in these texts recorded by ancient stargazers, but almost as impactful were the perspectives of those who considered their discoveries to be heresy. Any independent astronomer will find this an invaluable collection of titles arguing the truth of the cosmic system.

Early History of Industry & Science

Acting as a kind of historical Wall Street, this collection of industry manuals and records explores the thriving industries of construction; textile, especially wool and linen; salt; livestock; and many more.

Early English Wit, Poetry & Satire

The power of literary device was never more in its prime than during this period of history, where a wide array of political and religious satire mocked the status quo and poetry called humankind to transcend the rigors of daily life through love, God or principle. This series comments on historical patterns of the human condition that are still visible today.

Early English Drama & Theatre

This collection needs no introduction, combining the works of some of the greatest canonical writers of all time, including many plays composed for royalty such as Queen Elizabeth I and King Edward VI. In addition, this series includes history and criticism of drama, as well as examinations of technique.

Early History of Travel & Geography

Offering a fascinating view into the perception of the world during the sixteenth and seventeenth centuries, this collection includes accounts of Columbus's discovery of the Americas and encompasses most of the Age of Discovery, during which Europeans and their descendants intensively explored and mapped the world. This series is a wealth of information from some the most groundbreaking explorers.

Early Fables & Fairy Tales

This series includes many translations, some illustrated, of some of the most well-known mythologies of today, including Aesop's Fables and English fairy tales, as well as many Greek, Latin and even Oriental parables and criticism and interpretation on the subject.

Early Documents of Language & Linguistics

The evolution of English and foreign languages is documented in these original texts studying and recording early philology from the study of a variety of languages including Greek, Latin and Chinese, as well as multilingual volumes, to current slang and obscure words. Translations from Latin, Hebrew and Aramaic, grammar treatises and even dictionaries and guides to translation make this collection rich in cultures from around the world.

Early History of the Law

With extensive collections of land tenure and business law "forms" in Great Britain, this is a comprehensive resource for all kinds of early English legal precedents from feudal to constitutional law, Jewish and Jesuit law, laws about public finance to food supply and forestry, and even "immoral conditions." An abundance of law dictionaries, philosophy and history and criticism completes this series.

Early History of Kings, Queens and Royalty

This collection includes debates on the divine right of kings, royal statutes and proclamations, and political ballads and songs as related to a number of English kings and queens, with notable concentrations on foreign rulers King Louis IX and King Louis XIV of France, and King Philip II of Spain. Writings on ancient rulers and royal tradition focus on Scottish and Roman kings, Cleopatra and the Biblical kings Nebuchadnezzar and Solomon.

Early History of Love, Marriage & Sex

Human relationships intrigued and baffled thinkers and writers well before the postmodern age of psychology and self-help. Now readers can access the insights and intricacies of Anglo-Saxon interactions in sex and love, marriage and politics, and the truth that lies somewhere in between action and thought.

Early History of Medicine, Health & Disease

This series includes fascinating studies on the human brain from as early as the 16th century, as well as early studies on the physiological effects of tobacco use. Anatomy texts, medical treatises and wound treatment are also discussed, revealing the exponential development of medical theory and practice over more than two hundred years.

Early History of Logic, Science and Math

The "hard sciences" developed exponentially during the 16th and 17th centuries, both relying upon centuries of tradition and adding to the foundation of modern application, as is evidenced by this extensive collection. This is a rich collection of practical mathematics as applied to business, carpentry and geography as well as explorations of mathematical instruments and arithmetic; logic and logicians such as Aristotle and Socrates; and a number of scientific disciplines from natural history to physics.

Early History of Military, War and Weaponry

Any professional or amateur student of war will thrill at the untold riches in this collection of war theory and practice in the early Western World. The Age of Discovery and Enlightenment was also a time of great political and religious unrest, revealed in accounts of conflicts such as the Wars of the Roses.

Early History of Food

This collection combines the commercial aspects of food handling, preservation and supply to the more specific aspects of canning and preserving, meat carving, brewing beer and even candy-making with fruits and flowers, with a large resource of cookery and recipe books. Not to be forgotten is a "the great eater of Kent," a study in food habits.

Early History of Religion

From the beginning of recorded history we have looked to the heavens for inspiration and guidance. In these early religious documents, sermons, and pamphlets, we see the spiritual impact on the lives of both royalty and the commoner. We also get insights into a clergy that was growing ever more powerful as a political force. This is one of the world's largest collections of religious works of this type, revealing much about our interpretation of the modern church and spirituality.

Early Social Customs

Social customs, human interaction and leisure are the driving force of any culture. These unique and quirky works give us a glimpse of interesting aspects of day-to-day life as it existed in an earlier time. With books on games, sports, traditions, festivals, and hobbies it is one of the most fascinating collections in the series.

The BiblioLife Network

This project was made possible in part by the BiblioLife Network (BLN), a project aimed at addressing some of the huge challenges facing book preservationists around the world. The BLN includes libraries, library networks, archives, subject matter experts, online communities and library service providers. We believe every book ever published should be available as a high-quality print reproduction; printed on-demand anywhere in the world. This insures the ongoing accessibility of the content and helps generate sustainable revenue for the libraries and organizations that work to preserve these important materials.

The following book is in the "public domain" and represents an authentic reproduction of the text as printed by the original publisher. While we have attempted to accurately maintain the integrity of the original work, there are sometimes problems with the original work or the micro-film from which the books were digitized. This can result in minor errors in reproduction. Possible imperfections include missing and blurred pages, poor pictures, markings and other reproduction issues beyond our control. Because this work is culturally important, we have made it available as part of our commitment to protecting, preserving, and promoting the world's literature.

GUIDE TO FOLD-OUTS MAPS and OVERSIZED IMAGES

The book you are reading was digitized from microfilm captured over the past thirty to forty years. Years after the creation of the original microfilm, the book was converted to digital files and made available in an online database.

In an online database, page images do not need to conform to the size restrictions found in a printed book. When converting these images back into a printed bound book, the page sizes are standardized in ways that maintain the detail of the original. For large images, such as fold-out maps, the original page image is split into two or more pages

Guidelines used to determine how to split the page image follows:

• Some images are split vertically; large images require vertical and horizontal splits.
• For horizontal splits, the content is split left to right.
• For vertical splits, the content is split from top to bottom.
• For both vertical and horizontal splits, the image is processed from top left to bottom right.

THE RELATION BETWEENE

THE LORD OF A MANNOR AND THE COPPY-HOLDER His Tenant.

Delivered in the Learned Readings of the late Excellent and Famous Lawyer, Char. Cal-
throse of the Honorable Society of *Lincolnes-Inne* Esq;.

Whereby it doth appeare for what causes a Coppy-
holder may forfeite his Coppy-hold Estate,
and for what not : and likewise
what Lord can grant a
Coppy, and to *whom*.

Published for the good of the Lords of Mannors,
and their Tenants

Non magis pro manibus quam pro servandis legibus
liberi Cives pugnare debent, siquidem sine manibus
Respublica potest consistere sine Legibus non potest.

o

12.

LONDON:
Printed for *William Cooke*, and are to be sold at
his shop neere Furnivals Inne-gate in
Holborne. 1635.

March 24, 1847

COPPY HOLDS

The first Lecture.

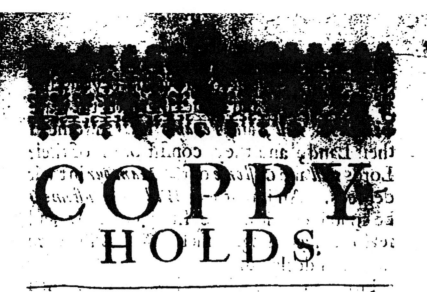

T H E great injuries which are offered, and small remedies which are used in cafes of Coppy-holds, which as it feemeth, doe grow by the obfcure knowledge what Law & Cuftome judgeth in thefe matters of Coppy-hold : moveth me to fhew fome part of my Travailes in thefe points, not thereby to animate Coppy-hold Tenants which would by too much advancing their Tenure, pretend only to be Tenants by Cuftome, and not Tenants at *Will*, nor to encourage any *Coppy-hold* Lord, which could by too much abafing thefe *Tenures*, pretend to have fuch *Coppy-*

B   *holders*

onely *Tenants* at *Will*, and not regard their cuſtomes, but to prove unto you, that as their Title, and name ſheweth they are *Tenants* at *will*, and *Tenants* by Cuſtome in their Land, and they conſiſt both of their Lords *will* and *Cuſtome* of the *Mannour* in their degrees. And that this *Will* and *Cuſtome* be contained within the Limits of Law and reaſon, according to ſuch rules as ſhall bee hereafter declared.

Firſt I wil ſhew what a Coppy-hold is, then whereof it doth conſiſt, and what eſtimation the ſame is of, by the Antiquity of time, and by the Lawes and Statutes of this Realme.

Maſter *Littleton* in his firſt book of *Tenures*, defineth a Tenant by Coppy of Court Role; and, to be where a man is ſeiſed of a *Mannour*, in which is a *Cuſtome* that hath been uſed time out of minde, that certaine Tenants of the ſame *Mannour* have uſed, to have certaine Lands and Tenements to hold to them and their heires, in Fee Simple, Fee Taile, or for Life at the will of the Lord after the Cuſtome of the Mannour : And that they have no other evidence but the Roles of the Court, by which definition, and by certaine other obſervations of the Law it may bee gathered, that a Coppy-hold doth conſiſt of theſe ſixe principall grounds, or Circumſtances. (*viz.*)

Firſt

First, there muſt be a *Mannour*, for the main-
tenance of *Coppyhold*.

Secondly, a cuſtome for the allowing of the
ſame.

Thirdly, there muſt be a Court holden for
the proofe of the Coppy-holders.

Fourthly, there muſt be a Lord to give the
Coppyhold.

Fittly, there muſt be a *Tenant* of capacity to
take the *Tenement*.

Laſtly, the thing to be Granted which
muſt bee ſuch as is Grantable, aud may bee
helde of the Lord according unto the *Tenure*.

But firſt before I ſpeake of theſe Circumſtances, I will briefly declare unto you the
Dignity and Eſtimation of *Coppyholders*,
by the Antiquity and allowance of time, and
by the Lawes and Statutes of this Realme.

It appeareth by a certaine Booke intituled
De priſcis anglor: legibus : Tranſlated out of
Saxon Tongue by Maſter *Lambert* of *Lincolns
Inne* ; that *Coppy-holds* were long before the
Conqueſt, and then called by the name of
(Bookeland) as you may ſee in the beginning
of the Booke, in the Treatiſe *De rerum
& verborum explicatione* ; and by Maſter
B R A C T O N an Auncient Writer of the
Lawes of E N G L A N D, who in
his Booke VVriteth divers preſidents

B 2   and

records of King *Henry* 3. of allowance
that Copyholders or *Customary tenants* doing
their due services, the Lord might not expell them; according to the Opinion of the
latter Iudges, in the time of *Edward* the 3.
and *Edward* the fourth : And it appeareth
by Master *Fitz-Herberts Abridgement*, they
were preserved by a *special Writ* for that purpose, and the Lord thereby compelled to do
right. And in the time of *Henry* the fourth,
Tenants by the Virge, which are the same
in Nature, as *Coppyholders* be, were allowed
by the name of *Sokemaines* in *Franktenure*,
& in the time of *Henry* 7. were allowed ayde
of the King, for defence of their estates. So
that in every Kings time *Coppy-holders* have
had their Allowances according unto their
Natures unto this present time : wherein our
Iustices are still of opinion, as the sayd grave
Sages have beene in times past. Now I will
further proceede in some particular use of
these Tenures, according to the Lawes and
Statutes of this Realme : And because I find
none that doth so much deface the estimation
of *Coppyholders*, as Master *Fitz-herbert* doth
in his Writ *De Recto clauso*. I will begin with
his words and iudgment in the same, and pro-
ceed to other Authorites.

Master *Fitz Herbert* sayth, that this Terme
Coppyholders is but a new Terme, newly
found

found out, & that in old time they were
Tenants in Vilenage, or bafe Tenure; and so
faith he, doth appeare in the old Tenures; for
no Coppy-holders are there fpoken of, although there were at that time fuch Tenants.
But then faith, they were called Tenants in
Vilenage, and faith, as appeareth 44. *Henry* 4.
If a falfe judgement be given againft them, in
the Lords Court, they fhall have no remedy,
but fue to their Lord by petition, becaufe to
hold by Coppy of Court Role, which is as
hee faith bafe Tenure, is to hold in Villenage, which faid opinion of *Fitz-Herbert*,
have beene by divers wrefted, to make no
diverfity betweene Tenure in Villenage, and
Tenure, by Coppy of Court Role or bafe Tenure, wherein whatfoever interpretation may
be made, Mafter *Fitz Herberts* meaning is
very plaine, and the Booke of the old Tenures, is to be farre otherwife underftood : as
alfo I fuppofe, all other Authorities in our
Law doe make and appoint difference betweene the faid Tenures. And firft touching
the Booke of the old Tenures it is plaine,
that the Booke maketh a plaine diftinction
betweene Tenure in Villenage, and *Tenure* in
Fee Bafe, which is underftood t' is *Tenure* by
Coppy hold, and calleth it a Fee, although
a bafe Fee, and maketh diverfe diftinctions
betweene them, and faith, that the *Tenants*

in *Villenage* muſt doe all ſuch things as their Lord will command them. But otherwiſe, it is of the *Tenants* in baſe Fee. And this it ſeemeth the ſayd Booke of old *Tenures* to be by Mr. *Fitzherbert* miſ-recited, which I am the bolder to affirme, ſaving the due reverence to his Learning : becauſe one Mr. *Thornton* of *Lincolns* Inne, a man very learned in his late Reading thereupon the *Statute* of *Forger de faits :* ſpeaking of *Forging Court Roles*, did plainely affirme the Booke of the old *Tenures* to bee miſtaken by Mr. *Fitzherbert* in this point. And beſides, for the further credit of *Coppy-holds*, wee ought to conſider the great Authority of Mr. *Littleton*, who amongſt the reſt of his *Tenures*, doth make a divided Chapter thereof, differing from the *Tenure* in *Villenage*, ſhewing there the Suites and Plaints of *Coppy-holders*, ſaying that they have an Eſtate of Inheritance according to the Cuſtome : And delivereth his owne opinion, that if a *Coppy-holder* doing his ſervices be expelled by the Lord, he ſhall have an Action of Treſpaſſe againſt his Lord : And ſaith that *Danby* and *Brian* 21. *Ed.* 4. were of the ſame minde, according to which is *Bracton*, and the ſayd Preſidents of *Hen.* 3. and the Writ uſed in *Tempore*, *R.* 2. beſides many other reaſons at the Common-Law, &c. prooving that by uſe and circumſtance things may alter and

change

change their originall nature.

As for example, the services of *Socage te-nure* was at the beginning, (as Mr. *Littleton* sayth) to Till the Lords Land, &c. And yet now by consent of the Lord, and by conti-nuance of time are turned into money, and o-ther Services in lieu thereof. Even so may be said of *Coppyholds*, as long as the *Tenants* themselves be free, though their *Tenure* were at beginning never so bound and base: yet by course of time, they may gaine moie liberty and freedome, and grow to more estimation and account. Another reason and Rule there is at the Common Law, to this intent, that some things there were which in the begin-ning were but *voluntary*, and yet in the end by continuance became *Compulsary*, as appeareth by the 27. *Aff. pla. 8. & Brook tit. præscrip. pla. 49. 27. Aff. præscrip. Brac.* That a man that did at the first of his own benevo'ence repaire a high way or a Bridge by often using to doe it, was afterwards compelled thereunto *volens nolens.* Even so it may be sayd of the *Coppy-holders*, who at the first held but at the free wil of the Lord; yet now by usage and conti-nualgranting time out of mind, they have got-ten an estate after the Custome, that doing their Services, and behaving themselves wel, they cannot by Law or Reason be deprived. Thus much for the allowance of *Coppy-hol-*

ders.

ders by the Common-Law , now let us con-
sider the Reputation of them by the Statutes
and Parliament Law.

It appeareth by the Statute of *1.Rich.3.ca.*
4. & *19. Hen.7. ca.* 16. That a *Coppy-holder*
that may dispend twenty sixe shillings eight
pence by the yeere shall be Empannelled on a
Iury, as he that may dispend twenty shillings
by the yeere of Free Lands. And by the Statute of the *2. Ed.6.cap.8.* the Interest of *Coppy-*
ders are reserved, being found by Office after
the death of the Kings Tenants, as well as o-
ther Estates at the Common-Law, and so doth
the Statute of Monasteries. *31. Hen.8. cap.13.*
& *1. Edw. 6. cap.* 14. preserve *Coppy holds*
from dissolving. And it will seeme that *Coppy-*
holders are for the good of the Common-
wealth, and therfore to be maintained, for that
some have bin erected and established by Parliament, which were not *demisible* by *Coppy* before, as appeareth by the Statutes *32.Hen.8.2.*
2. Ed.32.

What shall be said, a *Mannour*, and such a
Mannour as wil maintaine a Coppy-hold. A Mannour consisteth in two parts (*viz.*) Demeasnes
and Services, and neither of these two parts
hath the name of a Mannour without the o-
ther : for as a Messuage or Lands cannot be
called Demeasnes without Tenants thereunto belonging, to pay Rents and doe Services,

of Lands : So on the other part, though a
Man have Tenants ro pay him Rents, and
doe him Service, and no Messuage or Lands
whereupon to keepe his Court, and to receive
his Rents and Services, this cannot be called
a Mannor, but onely a Signiory in grosse,
Fitz. na. breu: f. 5. & 8.

Demeanes are so called, for that the Lord
himselfe occupieth and manureth them *In son*
maine Demeasne, but all Lands that have been
in the Lords owne hands, be not called *De-*
meanes, for all Free-holdes and Coppy-holds
were in his owne hands at the beginning. But
Demeanes is that which is now, and time out
of Mind have beene in the Lords hands, or
occupation of his Bayliffe or Servants : And
that also which auncient Coppy-hold may be
to some purpose called *Demeasnes*, because in
every Surrender in *Manus Domini*, and every
grant *extra manus Domini*, the Lord hath a
medling with it, and may thereupon keepe
his Court, and for the most part cut downe
Timber, and such like : And that is also
called *Demeasnes*, which now is in the Lords
hands by any new Escheate or forfeiture.
And also the Lands which are in the hands of
the Coppy-holders, and such a *Demeasne* as
with other Services will make a Mannour;

C   though

though the Lord hath none other demeanes
there in his owne hands, nor in the hands of
his Bayliffe, or servants such service, as with a
Demeasne shal make a *Mannour* to maintaine:
Coppy-holds is where a man holdeth Lands
or Tenements freely by suite to the Court of
the Lord of the *Mannour* within the said Fee:
But yet every kind of Service will not make a
Mannour, for Services are of two kinds, *viz.*
That is by Tenure and by covenant; Service
by Tenure is also of two sorts, as if a man
at this day giveth his Land in tayle, or leaseth it for Life or Yeares, saving the reversion: here is a Service of Fealty incident to
this Tenure, betweene the *Donor* or the
Lessor, and the *Donee* or the *Lessee*. And
yet though this be a Service by Tenure, yet
is it no such Service as will make a Mannour.
For if a man at this Day be seised of twenty
Acres of Land, and *infeffeth* nineteene severall persons of nineteene of these Acres, saving the twentieth to himselfe, and reserveth
of every of his *Feoffees* suite of the Court and
other Services to be done to this Court, to
be held on the twentieth Acre; though the
Feoffment be by Deed indented, or in tayle
or of Lives; yet all is voyde, land avayleth
not to make a Mannour. But it maketh onely
a Tenure ingrosse; for a Tenure may by di-

vers

vers meanes be created at this Day; but a
Mannour by no way, by a Common perfon.
Plow. Com. 2. 693.

A Mannour muft be by Prefcription, and
the Services by Continuance, time out of
mind.

But although a man at this Day cannot
make a Mannour; yet hee may in fome fort
enlarge a Mannour by adding more Services
unto it. 9. *Aff.* A man feifed of a Mannour
did give parcell of the fame to hold of him
by Suite to his Mill within the fame Mannour, for this Service the Lord may diftraine, and it is there held to bee accounted
parcell of the Mannour.

In like manner, a man may by referving
upon a gift, Intayle, or Leafe for Life: Services ingroffe, increafe the Services of an ancient *Mannour*. *Signior grant le Demeafnes*
& Services del fon Mannour de Norkelfey & foo
extend en auter Towne per le melior opinion des
Iuftices de Common Blank le grantee, &c. keepe
a Court there, and fo a *Mannour* to be created
at this Day.

What fhall be fayd by *Mannour* or a *Tenure*
in his proper nature or Common-Law, and

Pla. 24. Bro.
Tit. *Tenure.* 26

In the cafe of
Monfon and
Afton.

By the Report
of *Denham* of
Lincolns Inne

C 2   what

what in respect of Usage or Custome to maintaine Coppy-holds.

It is to be noted, that although a *Mannour* of his proper nature ought to consist of demeanes and Services, yet in some cases that may bee a Mannour, and maintaine Coppyholders, and a Court Baron; by usage and custome, which otherwise by Common Law is no Mannour, nor cannot so be called, &c.

A man seized of a Manour, whereunto be divers free Tenants, divers Coppy-holders, and divers speciall Customary Tenants; and the Customary Tenants, doe hold to give a tendance on the Free-holders at the Lords Court. All the Free Tenants dye saving one, the Lord doth bargain and sell the Manour to an Estranger: This is now in respect of the Free *Tenants*, a *Tenure*, and no Manour, in respect of the Coppy-holders, both a *Mannour*, and *Tenure*; and in respect of *Customary Tenants*, neither *Mannour*, nor *Tenure*.

If divers doe hold Lands, to dine with the Lord every Sunday in the yeare; this maketh neither good *Tenure*, nor *Mannour*.

But

But if they hold to wait on the Lord every Sunday at dinner, and to dine with him; this maketh a good service, but no good *Tenure*.

If divers doe hold Lands by *Coppy* of the *Mannour* of D. and so have done time out of minde, and by the like time there hath beene no Free-holders to the said Mannour, Although this be no *Mannour* in his proper nature, yet by usage it is a good *Mannour* to maintaine *Coppy-holds*.

A man seised of a *Mannour*, which time out of minde hath beene called by the name of the *Mannour* of S. and doth demise the same by the name of the *Mannour* of S. this is good.

If a man seised of a *Mannour*, whereto bee sixe Free-holders, and six Villaines Regardants: The Free-holders dye having issue sixe daughters, the Villaines enterrary with them, yet the same is a *Mannour*, and the villaines thereto regardant.

If a man seised of a *Mannour*, whereto he hath Leet, and wrecke of the sea by prescription, all the *Tenancyes* Escheate, yet the Leete and the wrecke still remaine, and it is a *Mannour* to that purpose.

If

If divers doe hold Lands by Prescription to find the Lords mans meate, and hounds meat, when he commeth to hunt the Fox in the said Lands; this maketh a good *Tenure*, but no good *Mannour*: If divers do hold lands to doe suit and service at the Lords Court, This is most properly such service as maketh a *Mannour*: but if it be to doe suit and Service at the Lords Court, when it pleaseth themselves, this is neither *Mannour* nor *Tenure*. If divers doe hold Lands to repaire a High way within a mile compasse, without the bounds of the Lord of the *Mannour*, this makes a good *Tenure*, but no *Mannour*. But to repaire or mend the wayes within the Precinct of the *Mannour*, is good to enlarge the *Mannour*.

If divers doe hold Lands to pray for the prosperous Estate of the Lord and his Heires; this maketh a *Tenure*, but no good *Mannour*.

If divers doe hold Lands of the Lord to waite upon him at twenty dayes warning, twenty miles distant from the *Mannour*; this maketh a good Service, but no good *Tenure*. But if it bee to waite upon the Lord within the said *Mannour*, by certaine space, this

this maketh both a good *Tenure*, and a good *Mannour*.

If divers hold Lands to beate or kill the Lords Tenants that shall doe Trespasse on the Lords *Demeasnes*, this is neither good *Tenure*, nor good *Mannour*. But if it be to beate and kill the Kings enemies, that shall doe so, this maketh both a good *Tenure*, and a good *Mannour*.

If divers hold Lands by Prescription to doe Service to the Lord, to his Court of the said *Mannour*, twenty miles distant at a place certaine. This is both a good *Tenure* and a good *Mannour*. But if it be to doe Service to his Court at another *Mannour*, this without Prescription, cannot be severante from the first *Mannour*.

If Divers doe hold to come to the Lords Court, and there to doe nothing, this maketh neither good *Tenure* nor good *Mannour*. But to come to the Court, though not to be of the Homage, yet to afferre *Amerciaments*, or make *Certificates*, or any other Service to the Lord, this maketh a good *Tenure* and a *Mannour*.

If any do hold Lands to doe Divine Service
before

before the Lord and his Tenants in the
Court-house, before the beginning of every Court, this maketh both a good *Tenure*
and a good *Mannour*. *What shall be said, a
good Custome to bee able to maintaine Coppy-
hold.*

A Custome to make a Coppy-hold, must
be of necessity in the same Mannour, where
the said Coppy-holds are so granted, *viz.*
That the same Lands are, and time out of
minde have beene onely Demised and demisable by Coppy of Court Role: for otherwise the Lord cannot grant it by Coppy, because he cannot beginne a Custome at this
Day. But if it have beene by like time granted by Coppy, though sithence it came to the
Lords hands, yet if the Lord never *Demise*
the same by *Free Deede* nor otherwise, but by
Coppy, then he may well grant againe the
same by *Coppy*, for it is neither the person
of the Lord, nor the occupation of the
Land, that either maketh or marreth the
Coppy-hold: But onely the usage and manner
of *Demising* the same, for the prescription of
a *Coppy-holder* consisteth neither in the Land,
nor in the Occupier, but onely in the Usage.

The

THE DIVISION OF CVSTOMES.

viz.

{ Cuftomes,
Prefcriptions.
Vfage, and
Limitation.

THefe foure though t'ey be by fome con- The devifion founded together, and indeede are of of Cuftomes. great Affinity ; yet there be divers differences in their feverall natures betweene them.

Cuftome is where by continuance of time, a Right is obtained concerning divers perfons in common.

Prefcription is where by continuance of time one particular perfon obtaineth Right againft another.

Vfage is by continuance of time the efficient caufe of them both.

D   *Limitation*

Limitation is where a right may be obtai-
red, by reafon of a *non* claime, by the fpace
of a certaine number of yeeres, differing in the
Accompt of time, from cuftome and prefcription.

But what meafure of time fhall make a
Cuftome; divers have differed in opinion;
fome judging the fame to bee according to
the Computation of yeeres, from the time
of K. *Hen.* 1. untill the Statute of *Merton ca.*8.
which appointeth the limitation in a writ of
right: The accompt of which time unto the
faid Statute, from the faid K. time is 76.
yeares, others have thought a hundred
yeeres was accompted a Fee fimple.

But the true meafure thereof according to
Mafter *Littletons* Rule, is where a Cuftome,
or Ufage, or other things have beene ufed, fo
long as a mans memory cannot remember the
contrary. That is, when fuch matter is pleaded, that no man then in life, hath not
heard any thing, nor know any proofe to the
contrary.

And by this it appeareth that *Cuftomes*, and
prefcriptions, refteth onely in the memory
of

of man, & limitation confifteth only of a certaine time, which hath a certaine beginning and of certaine ending, and is not directed by mans memory, wherein is ment limitation of time, and not limitation of eftates.

If Lands have beene demifed by Coppy by the fpace of 60. yeeres, and yet there be fome alive, that remembreth the fame occupied by Indenture, this is not a good Coppy-hold.

And if Lands have beene demifed by Coppy but 40. yeeres, and there is none alive that can remember the fame to bee otherwife demifed: This is a good Coppy-hold, for the number of yeeres makes not the matter, but the memory of man. And it is not 60. 80. or 100. yeeres that maketh a Coppyhold or a cuftome, though it makes a limitation. But fuch certaine number of yeeres makes onely a likely-hood, or prefumption of a prefcription; that is, that it commonly happneth not that any mans memory alive, can remember alone fuch a number of yeeres. But if any chance to be alive, that remembreth the contrary, then fuch prefcription muft give place to fuch proofe.

Cuftome hath certaine fpeciall vertues in

it

it felfe, which for the more eftimation thereof, I will fhortly fhew according to certaine
precepts and principals allowed by all **Laws**,
both by the Law of God, the Law of Nature, and the Law of Nations, and by the
private Law of every Countrey : as by the
Law of G O D it is faid, *Si quis videtur con-*
tentiofus effe nos talem Confuetudinem non ha-
bemus ,nec ecclefia Dei, which proveth that the
Scripture and the Church of God do attribute
fomewhat to good cuftomes, though not to
evill : And by the Law of Nature, *Confuetudo*
eft altera natura. And by the Law of Nations, *Confuetudo eft optima legum interpres.*
And by the Lawes of this Realme, Princes
at their Coronation are fworne, as well to
keepe the cuftome of this Land, as the Lawes
of this Land, which Law doth attribute fo
much to cuftome, that fometimes it is admitted to derogate from the Common Law,
for *Confuetudo bona de caufa ufitata et appro-*
bata, privat communem Legem.

Where

WHEREOF CVSTOME
doth Confift.

CUstome although it doth chiefly con-
fift of continuance of time and ufage,
yet it doth further require feven other
neceffary properties, incident for the main-
tenance of a good Cuftome : Which are
thefe.

FIrft, it muft be reafonable, as it appeareth
2. *Ed.* 4. 24.

SEcondly, it muft be certaine, as appeareth
3. *Ed.* 3. 13. *Ed.* 3. 4.
*Dum fuit infra ætatem.*3.14.*Ed.*3.4.14.*H.*4

THirdly, it muft be according to Common right. 42. *Ed.* 3. 4.

FOurthly, it muft be on good confiderati-
on. 5. *Hen.* 7.9. *Bro. tit. prefcr pcon pla.*57
22. *Affi pla.* 58.

FIftly, it muft bee compulfary. 42. *Ed.* 3.
Avow 66.

Sixtly,

SIxtly, it muſt be without prejudice to the King. 3. *Hen.* 6. Cuſtome *Fits. Hen.* 5. 22. *Ed.* 3. Preſcription. 40.

SEventhly, it muſt bee to his profit that claimeth the ſame. 31. *Ed.* 3. Preſcription 40. *et* 28.

Uſage is the efficient cauſe, both of Cuſtome and Preſcription ; for without uſage, there can bee neither *Cuſtome* or Preſcription, for even as the minde is to man, ſo is uſage to *Cuſtome.* And as you ſee there bee divers varieties of minds in men, ſo are there many varieties of *Cuſtomes* as you ſee varieties of Countries, and yet all men perfect, and all *Cuſtomes* perfect: ſome ſay that men have their minds affected according to the Conſtitution of their bodies : And ſo have *Countries* their *Cuſtomes,* according to the *conſtitution* of the places, as in *Kent,* and in North-*Wales,* becauſe thoſe *Countries* have beene moſt ſubject to forraigne invaſions, (that every man there, may bee of power for reſiſtance.) The inheritance for the noſt part deſcend in gavell kind (*viz.*) to every brother alike, and in other middle parts of the Realme for whoſe government. *Leaſt equality is beſt.*

The

The inheritance wholly defcendeth to the eldeft brother: And in *Borough* Englifh which is in divers *Boroughs*, becaufe their fubftance commonly is Lands, and in fuch Townes, Lands may bee the better preferved then goods, therefore their youngeft fonnes fhal onely have their Lands : and as it is in thofe great parts of the Realme, fo it is in divers private parts and Mannors, and divers private and fpecial cuftomes. As fome Mannors have Coppy-hold of inheritance, fome for life, or lives : in fome Manour the Copy-holders furrender in one manner, and in fome in another fort : In fome the Fine is Arbitrable : And in fome certaine, *et fic in fimilibus*.

The ufage of every Cuftome doth not reft to be yeerely, dayly, or continually ufed, but as the equality, and the nature of the thing whereof the Cuftome is, doth require, as Cuftome *Harryots* when they fall, of Shacts and Eoldage, in their feafon of Common of Eftovers in their time, and for Coppy-holders whofe Fines are certaine, yet at one time to pay a greater Fine than at another, and all thefe are good Cuftomes, though they cannot bee ufed at all times, for Cuftomes may bee fometimes ufed, fometimes

nor

not ufed, fometimes altered, and fometimes not, and therefore in *Cuſtome* you may fee there is (*uſer*, *non uſer*) Abuſer and interuſer.

Uſer is, when according to time and occaſion a *Cuſtome* is uſed.

Non uſer is when for want of time and occaſion, or through negligence, or forgetfulneſſe a *Cuſtome* is not uſed.

Abuſer is that, when *Cuſtome* is ill uſed; for as Uſer doth nouriſh *Cuſtome*, ſo doth Abuſer deſtroy a *Cuſtome*; and yet in ſome caſes a *Cuſtome* may be ſometimes uſed in one ſort, and ſometimes in another. And yet a good *Cuſtome*, if there bee good conſiderations of the exchanging thereof at times, and this I call enteruſer,

If there be a *Coppy-hold*, of an Ancient demeaſne, and this Land is forfeited to the Lord by waſte, and thereupon a ſeiſure awarded thereof, and yet the Lord doth ſuffer the Tennant ſtill to occupy it, by the ſpace of 20. yeeres, without receiving any Rent for the ſame, and after grants the ſaid Land

to the Tenant by Coppy. This grant is good and a good Ufer of the *Coppy-hold*. But if after the faid *feafure* awarded, an *Eftranger* had entred, and Diffeifed him of his Land, and made a *Feofment* in *Fee* thereof; And after the Lord re-entreth, and grants the fame againe by Coppy unto the firft Tenant. This grant is not good, by reafon of the Ufer of this Land.

If the Lord have ufed at the admiffion of his *Coppy-hold Tenants*, fometime to take for a Fine two-pence, or fometimes foure-pence for an Acre, fometimes twelvepence an Acre, this Ufer is fo uncertaine, that it maketh the Fine arbitrable at the Lords will.

If the Lord of a *Mannor* have ufed time out of mind, to admit his *Coppy-hold Tenants* without Fine, this ufage fhall binde the Lord, as well as a Fine certaine.

If the Lord have ufed to have certaine work-dayes of his Tenants, and that hath not beene ufed by the fpace of twenty yeares laft paft; yet that *non-ufer* is no difcharge to the *Tenants*, fo that there be any in life that can remember the fame.

If the Tenants have ufed when they fow their Lands, to pay the Lord Rent-corne, and when it lyeth in pafture to pay their rents in Money, this is a good Inter-ufer.

E   If

If the Tenants have used to pay to their Lord every fourth yeare a double Rent, and every sixt yeare an halfe Rent, this is a good Inter-user.

If the Tenants have used to have Common of Pasture in their Lords Woods, for their Horse-Cattell, and they put in their Neate-Cattell, and destroy the Woods, this is an abuser. But it is but Fineable, and no forfeiture of the *Common*, which they might have rightfully used: No more then if they have Common for a certaine number of Beasts in the Lords Soyle, and they will exceede the number; this abuse by their Surcharging, is onely fineable, and not Forfeiture.

If a man have a Market to be used one Day in a Weeke, the *non-user* thereof is not forfeiture. And if a man have a Market to bee used on the *Friday*, and hee keepeth the same *Friday* and *Munday*, the Mis-user of the *Munday* is no forfeiture of the *Friday*.

If a Man have a Faire to be used two daies and he keepes it three dayes, this abuse is a Forfeiture.

If a man have a Faire for one Day, and he will

will keepe it two dayes, and that is prefented to the *Exchequer*: If the party being called by *Proceffe*, doth claime both dayes by
Patent, upon fight whereof it appeares hee
ought to have but one day by his Patent, and
the other by *Prefcription*, though the Prefcription bee found againft him, and that
Day loft, yet he fhall enjoy the other Day.

If a man prefcribe to have a Faire yearely
upon *Bartholmew day*, and if the fame doe
fall out on the Sunday, then to keepe the
fame the next day following, this is a good
Prefcription.

If the King doe grant to the Citizens of
Norwich the *Franchifes* and *Liberties* that
London hath, and the *Franchifes* and *Liber-
ties* that *Southampton* hath: if the Citizens of
Norwich doe abufe one of thefe *Liberties* that
London hath; this is a forfeiture of all thofe
Liberties that *London* hath, and of no other.
But if the King doth incorporate a Towne,
and give them by the fame Patent Speciall
Franchifes and *Liberties*, the abufer of the
one of thefe, is a forfeiture of them all.

E 2   *THAT*

THAT EVERY CVSTOME
must bee reasonable ; and what
shall be said, *A reasonable*
Custome.

EVery good *Custome* is grounded upon
good *Reason*, and that shall bee said in
Reason a good *Custome*, that in reason is a
good Law, for *Law* and *Custome* be of that
affinity, as both doth allow like reason, and
both doth forbid like inconveniences. And
the finall effect of both to discusse and to dis-
cerne every mans true right, and to give to
every man that which is his owne. For although *Custome* in some cases differ from
Law, and doth admit execution of some
Acts without some ceremonies and circum-
stances bee required by the Law : yet the
end and effect of Custome is to maintain the
like reason that Law doth, and to avoyd the
like inconveniences.

And therefore if a Lord will *Prescribe* to
have

have such a Custome within his *Mannor*, that if the *Beasts* of any of his *Tenants* do him any Trespasse upon any of his *Demeasnes*, and there be taken *damage feasant*, that then hee may detaine them untill the owner shall satisfie him for his harmes, as himselfe shall require. This is no reasonable Custome that he should be his owne Judge. But to *Prescribe*, that if any of the Coppy-holders beasts Trespasse, &c. and the same be presented at his Court, that there should be a forfeiture of his Coppy-hold, this may be called a reasonable Custome.

If Tenants of a Mannour will *Prescribe* to hold without paying any Rents or Services for their Coppy-holds, this is no good Custome. But to *Prescribe* to hold by Fealty for all manner of Services, is good and reasonable.

If the Lord will *Prescribe* never to hold a Court, but when it pleaseth himselfe, this is not good. But to *Prescribe* never to hold a Court for the speciall good of any one Tenant, except the same Tenant will pay him a fine for the same, is good and allowable.

THAT

THAT EVERY

Cuſtome ought to be certaine; and what ſhall be ſaid, a Cuſtome certaine.

THere is nothing more required in all
Lawes and Cuſtomes, then certainty; for
incertainty in all caſes maketh confuſion, and
therfore Law and Cuſtome doth alſo agree in
this poynt, that without ſome kinde of certainty, neither *Law* nor *Cuſtome* can be good:
for in divers caſes, where one thing may bee
taken to divers intents, and the circumſtances
of the caſe ſuch as to which intent the thing
was done, cannot bee certainly judged, there
the ſame thing ſo doubtfully done, ſhall to
all purpoſes be judged voyde. And incertainty of *Cuſtomes* and *cuſtomary* cauſes, grows
chiefly three manner of waies. That is to
ſay, ſometimes of the incertainty of the Perſons: Sometime the incertainty of the things;
and ſometimes the incertainty of the cauſe:
and in ſome of theſe caſes, though there
bee

be at the firſt a Semblance of incertainty; yet by Circumſtances and Contingents, the incertainties may be turned into Certainties. As if the Lord of the Mannour will preſcribe that whenſoever any of his Coppy-holders dye without heires, that one other of the Coppy-holders of the ſame Mannor ſhal Till the Land for the yeare following. This is no good Cuſtome, becauſe the intent neither is, nor can be certaine, which of the Tenants ſhall performe this Service.

But if the *Cuſtome* be, that if a Coppy-holder dye without heire, that then the eldeſt Tenant of that name, of the ſaid Mannour, ſhall have this Land ; this is a good *Cuſtome*, and containeth in it ſelfe ſufficient certainty.

If a Coppy-holder do Surrender two Acres of Land into the Lords hand, the one to the uſe of *I. S.* and the other to the uſe of *I.N.* and doth not name in certainty who ſhal have the one Acre, and who ſhall have the other, the limitation of this uſe is voyd, for this incertainty.

If a Coppy-hold be ſurrendred to the uſe of *I.S.* and his Heires, untill hee ſhall

marry

marry *A. G.* and after the said marriage,
then to the use of them two in taile speciall,
if after they doe marry, then is the Surrender to them in taile, and till then, to him in
Fee.

If the Lord will prescribe to have of his
Coppy-holders in the time of peace two-
pence an Acre of Rent, and in the time of
Warre foure pence an Acre of Rent, this is
good *Prescription*, because there is a good
consideration of the cause of this incertaine-
ty : But to pay unto the Lord two-pence
an Acre rent when hee will, and foure-
pence an Acre Rent when hee will, this is
no good *Prescription*, because there is neither good reason nor consideration hereof,
nor can it ever be reduced into any certainty.

THAT

THAT CVSTOME MVST
bee according to Common Right :
And what shall be said such a
Custome, and what not.

CUstomes and Prescriptions must bee according to common right, that is to prescribe, to have such things as is their right,
and reason, to have, and not by custome of
Prescription to claime things by way of ex-
tortion, or thereby to exact Fines or other
things of his Tenant without good cause, or
consideration.

42. *Henry* 4.
Avowry 66.14
Her. 4. *Beben.*

If the Lord will prescribe to have of every
of his Coppy-holders, for every *Court* that
shall bee kept upon the Mannour a certaine
sum of money; this is no prescription according to common right, because he ought for
Justice sake to doe it *gratis.*

And so it is if the Shriefe will prescribe

F   to

to have a certaine Fee, for keeping his Turne, this is not a good prescription.

But if the Lord will prescribe to have a certaine Fee of his Tennants for any extraordinary Court purchased, onely for the benefit of one Tennant, as for one Tennant to take his Coppy-hold, or such like, this is a good prescription according to the common right.

Com. Little.
plac. 21.2 et
Yaxley 5. H 7
19.B2R.3.16
13. Hen. 7.16
D.St.47.2.
Ed.4.17.

If the Lord will have of any of his Tenants that shall commit a pound Breach, a hundred shillings for a Fine, this is good *Prescription*, but to challenge of every stranger that shall commit a Pound Breach a hundred shillings, this is no good prescription.

If the Lord will *Prescribe* that every of his Coppy-holders within his Mannour that shall marry his Daughter without licence shall pay a Fine to the Lord; this is no good *Prescription* according to common right.

THAT

THAT A CVSTOME
muſt be upon a good Conſideration, and what ſhall be
*ſaid ſuch a Cuſtome, and
what not.*

COnſideration hath a great effect in all
Lawes and Cuſtomes, and hath as great
an operation, as any one thing belonging to
the Law, for in moſt cauſes it onely guideth
and directeth Rights, properties, uſes, and e-
ſtates, ſometimes according to the limitation,
and ſometimes contrary to the limitation,
as well in caſes of *Cuſtome*, as in caſes of
common Law, for conſideration is the beginning of all Cuſtome, the ground of all
uſes, the reaſon of all rights, and the cauſe
of all duties : For without Conſideration no
Cuſtome can have continuance ; nothing is
wrought by any conveyance, no intereſt
transferred, no right remooved, no pro-
perty changed, nor duty accrewed. As if the
Lord of a Mannour will preſcribe, that who-
ſoever paſſeth the Kings high way , which

lyeth

lyeth through his Mannour, shall pay to the
Lord of the Mannour twelve-pence for his
passage. This prescription is not upon good
Consideration: But if hee prescribe to have
a penny of every one that passeth over such
a Bridge, which the Lord of the Mannour
doth use to repaire, this is a good prescription, and upon good consideration. If the Lord
will prescribe to have a Fine at the Marriage
of his Coppy-hold Tenants, in which the
Custome doth not admit the husband to bee
Tenant by courtesie, nor the Wife to be Tenant in Dowre, or have her Widdowes e-
state; the prescription of such a Fine is not
good: But in such Mannour where the cu-
stom doth admit such particular estates, there
a prescription for a Fine at the Marriage
of his coppy-holders, is upon good consideration.

Ifa coppy-holder surrender his Land to the
use of I. S. so long as I. S. shall serve him in
such an office; if I. S. refuse to serve, his e-
state doth cease.

If a coppy-holder doth surrender his
Land to the use of a stranger, in consideration that the same stranger shall marry his
daughter before such a day: if the marriage
succeeds

succeeds not, the stranger takes nothing by the Surrenderer: But if the Surrender bee in consideration, that the stranger shall pay such summe of money, at such a day ; though the money bee not payed, yet the Surrenderer standeth good.

If the Coppy-holder in consideration of twenty pounds to bee paid by I. S doth make a surrender of his Land to N. R. this Surrender is to the use of I. S. because of the consideration, expressed in the Coppy, and not to the use of N. R. But if in the Coppy the use bee expressed to N. R. and no consideration mentioned, the use expressed shall stand against any consideration to be averred.

THAT

THAT A CVSTOME MVST

be compulfary; and what fhall be faid fuch a Cuftome, and what not:

Cuftome or Law muſt be **Compulfary**, and not at the liberty of a man, whether hee will performe it or not; for then it were of no force; for all Cuſtomes and Lawes have their effect in two points. That is, in bidding that which is juſt, and in forbidding the contrary: So that the Lawes and Cuſtomes are reſtrainers of liberties, and doe demaund execution of Juſtice; not that every man ſhould have, or doe what they would; but that which by Juſtice they ought, whereunto by duty of Law and Cuſtome, hee is compellable; for otherwiſe it were Voluntary in him, which were to the infringing of the Law and good order: As the Poëts,

Oderunt peccare boni virtutis amore,
Oderunt peccare mali formidine pœnæ.

It

If the Lord will *prescribe* that every of his Tenants shall give him ten shillings a moneth, to beare charges in time of Warre; this is no good *Prescription*. But to prescribe that they ought to pay ten shillings, a moneth &c. this is good. For payment is *compulsary*, but gift is *Voluntary*.

If a Coppy-holder doe Surrender his Land to the use of *I. S.* so that the said *I. S.* doe pay him twenty pounds at such a day. If *I. S* please to pay the same, this is an absolute Surrender, and not conditionall, because the payment is *compulsary*.

But many Customes there are which at the beginning were Voluntary, and now by continuance are growne *Compulsary*. According to the Civill Law. *Quæ initio fuerunt voluntatis, ex post facto fuerunt necessitatis;* which also agreeth with the Common-Law in many *cases*, as I have partly touched before.

THAT

THAT A CVSTOME MVST

be without preiudice to the King, and
by what prescription the King shall
be bound, and what not.

THE King hath that Prerogative over his Subjects, that he is not tyed to time as a common person is, for though a common person may *loose* his right by *non* claime within a certaine time, the Kings right is still to be *preserved*, for *Nullum tempus occurrit Regi.* Yet in *speciall cases* where the King is not Intituled against such *prescription* by matter of Record, there such Customes shall bind the King.

As for example, if a Coppy-holder *prescribeth* that he holdeth of the King by Coppy, this is good; and by fine certaine, and not arbitrable: to have Waife and Strayes, and Wrecke (but not *Cattalla felonum aut fugitorum,*) and *utlagatorum* without Charters.

The Kings *Advowson* shall never fall into lapse for not *presenting* within sixe Moneths.

THAT

THAT A CVSTOME OVGHT
to consist of perdurablenesse of Estate, and of an able capacity.

TO those former parts whereuppon I have declared a good Custome to consist, may be added to either parts, *viz*. That he which will claime by Custome, must have a sufficient and perdurable estate to *prescribe* ; And also in his owne right, or in some others, a sufficient ability or capacity to *prescribe*.

Touching the first, it is to be understood that hee, which will *prescribe*, must have a certaine and undefeazable estate, and not otherwise. As if a *Tenant* at Will, or at sufferance, after hee hath occupyed the Land for ten yeares, will *prescribe* to have the same for ten yeeres more, this is not good. But a *Tenant* at Will after the Custome, although hee came in at the first by the Lords wil, yet doing and paying that which he ought, he may *prescribe* to hold the Land whether the Lord will or no : And although a Coppy-holder may *prescribe* in this forme against his Lord,

G   yet

yet againſt an Eſtranger, for a common or
ſuch like kind of profit, hee cannot *preſcribe*,
but in the right of the Lord : neither yet can
a Tenant for life, or for yeeres, *preſcribe* in
the right of their owne Eſtate onely, becauſe
it lacketh continuance to make a *cuſtome* or
preſcription (except) in ſome caſes of neceſſi-
ty, the Lord of a *Mannour*, or of a Patronage
for yeeres or life, may grant a Coppy in per-
petuity or *preſentation* for a longer time than
the eſtate of the Grantor doth continue, and
this is admitted *cauſa neceſſitatis*, and not
Iure preſcriptionis.

To the ſecond, Capacity muſt be in himſelfe that doth *preſcribe* ; which ability and
Capacity muſt conſiſt in the perſon of him
that doth *preſcribe* : For as *preſcription* may
be ſometimes in reſpect of eſtate, *Mannour*,
Lands, or *Offices* ; ſo may *preſcription* ſometimes be in reſpect of *perſon*, which *perſon* is
not to be underſtood of a private perſon ; but
of a body Politicke, not that many *perſons*
may *preſcribe*, except the ſame bee incorporate ; and to *preſcribe* in reſpect of their incorporate capacity, and not in reſpect of
their private capacity. As if the Inhabi-
tants of *Dale* will *preſcribe* to have Common
in the Soyle of S. this is no good *preſcription* ;
for

for that they be not incorporate, they muſt *preſcribe* that *H.* Lord of the *Mannour* of *Dale*, for him and his Tenants within the ſaid *Mannour*, have uſed to have Common within the ſaid Soyle: ſo is it for Coppy-holders, for they muſt *preſcribe* in the name of their Lord in ſuch a *caſe*.

If a man preſcribe that hee and his Anceſtors have had ſuch an Annuity, this is not good : But if a Biſhop doe preſcribe that hee and his predeceſſors have had ſuch an annuity this is good.

The pleading of *Preſcription* muſt bee uſed in forme of Law, as other matters that be pleadable, and forme muſt be uſed (likewiſe) in pleading of Coppy-holds, and other Cuſtomary Titles for avoyding of confuſion and diſcord; as well as in other caſes of the Common Law, the forme of pleading preſcription doth differ as the quality of the thing, whereof *preſcription* is made, and ſome times doth differ, as the perſons doe differ which make the *preſcription*: As if a Coppyholder makes his Title to his land by *preſcription*; he muſt plead that the ſame Land is, and hath beene time out of mind *Demiſed* and *Demiſeable*, by the Coppy of Court rolé, according to the cuſtome of the *Mannour* whereof it is holden.

If

If two men as younger brethren will make
their Title to Land in *Gavell kinde*, they muft
fay, that the fame Land is of the *Tenure* and
Nature of *Gavell kinde*, which time out of
minde, have bin parted and partable between
Heires males.

So if the youngeft Sonne maketh his Title
to Land in Borough Englifh, hee muft plead,
that time out of minde, the *Cuftome* of the faid
Mannour hath bin, that when, or at what time
foever a Coppy-holder dyeth *Seifed of* any
Coppy-hold Lands in the fame *Mannour*, having divers Sonnes, that the fame hath ufed
Iure Hereditario, to defcend unto the youngeft Sonne, &c.

And as the forme doth differ in the things
whereof the *Prefcription* is commonly made,
fo doth it differ as the Perfons do differ, which
prefcribe as a private perfon fhall *prefcribe* in
him and his Anceftors, whofe eftate he hath.
An incorporate perfon in him and his Prede-
ceffors. A Lord of a *Mannour* in him and them
which were Lords of that *Mannour*.

A Sheriffe, in him and thofe which have
beene Sheriffes of the fame County.

A Steward of a *Mannour* in him and thofe
which have beene Stewards there.

A

A Free holder in him and them which have beene Stewards to the said Lord.

A Coppy-holder shall *prescribe* against an Estranger, that the Lord of the Mannour, for him and his Tenants at will, have used the like,&c.

WHAT NECESSITY A

Court Baron is of, whereof it doth consist, how it is defined, and what shall be said a suffi- cient Court Role to make a Coppy-hold.

Every Manour hath a *Court* Baron inci- dent to it, of common right, and com- mon necessity, and this *Court* Baron con- sisteth of foure speciall parts, *viz*. The Lord, the Steward, the Tenants, and the Bayliffe.

A *Court* Baron is defined to bee an assem- blie of these parts together, within the said Mannour, to take *Councell*, care, and enquire of caufes concerning the fame Mannour: to fee juftice duely executed, the acts and ordinances there done to bee recorded in the Roles of the fame *Court*, which Roles are the evidence of all ordinances, duties, cuftomes, and conveyances betweene the Lord and Tennants of the faid Mannour, and are to bee entred by the Steward or an Officer indifferent betweene the Lord and his Tennants, and the fame Roles to remaine with the Lord, thereby to know his Tennants, his Rents, and his Fines, his Cuftomes, and his fervices.

And the particular grant of every *Coppyhold*, to bee coppyed out of the Roles, the coppyes thereof to bee delivered to every particular Tennant, neither can they make any other Title to their faid Tennements, but by their faid *Coppy*.

If the Lord of the Mannour having *Coppy-hold* Lands Surrendred into his hands, will in the prefence of his Tennants out of the *Court*, grant the fame to another, and the Steward entreth the fame into the Court-Booke, and maketh thereof a Coppy to the grantee, and the Lord dye before the next Court, this is no good Coppy to hold the Land.

But if the fame Surrender, and grant be prefented at the next Court, in the life of the Lord, and the grantee admitted Tenant, and a Coppy made to him, this is a good Coppy.

If the Lord of a Mannour having ancient Coppy-hole in his hands, will by a deed of Feofment, or by a Fine grant this Land to one to hold at the will of the Lord, according to the Cuftome, yet this cannot make a good Coppy-hold.

If the Lord in open Court doth grant a Coppy-hold Land, and the Steward maketh no entry thereof in the Court Roles, this is not good, though it bee never fo publicke done, nor no Collaterall proofe can make it good.

But if the Tenant have no Coppy made unto him out of the Role, or if hee loofe his *Coppy*, yet the Roles is ftill a fufficient tytle for his *Coppy-hold*, if the Roles bee alfo loft, yet it feemeth that by proofe

hee

hee can make this good.

If Ordinances or by Lawes bee newly made, and Recorded in the Roles of the
Court, if the Court Roles bee loft, the by
Lawes be fet at liberty, yet if there be any ancient cuftomes or priviledges by *Prefcriptions*
not entred in the Roles, &c. though the
Roles be loft, yet they remaine good.

WHO SHALL BE SAID
fuch a Lord of a Mannour as
hath power to grant a
Coppy hold.

A Lord to grant or allow a Coppy-hold,
muft be fuch a one, as by *Littletons* definition is feifed of a Mannour, fo that he muft
be in poffeffion at the time of the grant, for
although he have good right and title, yet if
he be not in poffeffion of the Mannour, it will
not ferve: and on the other fide, if hee bee in
poffeffion of the Mannour, though he have
neither

neither right nor title thereunto, yet in many cafes the grant and allowance of fuch a *Coppy*, is good as *Dominus de facto, fed non de iure*. And in fome cafes a *Coppy hold* fhall be adjudged good, according to the largeneffe of the ftate of the Lord that granted the fame, and in fome cafes fhall continue good for a longer time than the eftate of the granter was at the time of the grant. But that is to be underftood in cafe of neceffity, otherwife it will not be allowed.

If a man feifed of a Mannour, in which are divers *Coppy-holds* demifeable for lives, is diffeifed, and the diffeifor granteth a *Coppy-hold*, being voide, for three lives; this is not good to binde the diffeifed, other-wife it is of a Coppy-hold of Inheritance, becaufe it is neceffary to admit the next heire.

If a man have a Title to enter into a Mannour for a condition broken, and he granteth a *Coppy-hold* of the fame Mannour (being void) at a *Court* Baron, this is a good grant, for the keeping of the *Court* amounteth to an entre into the Mannour.

A man feifed of a Mannour for life,

H   where-

whereunto bee Coppy-hold of Inheritance belonging, and one Coppy-holder Surrendreth to the ufe of a ftranger in Fee, the Lord may grant this in Fee, and this Grant fhall binde him in the reverfion; but if the Coppy-holds being demifable for lives, it is otherwife, for then hee cannot upon Surrender grant the fame, longer than the life of the Grantor. But if the Lord of a Mannour for yeeres, or during the minority of a Ward, of which the Coppy-holds are demifable for three lives fucceffively, and not furvivingly; in this cafe if the Coppy-holder dyeth, the Lord may grant the fame, being voide for three lives, at his pleafure, and this fhall binde him in the Reverfion, or the heire at his full age.

WHO

WHO SHALL BE SAID
such a Tenant as may be a
COPPY-HOLDER.

ALthough there feemeth fome fhew of difference betweene Coppy-holders, and Cuftomary Tenants, yet differ not they fo much in nature, as in name; for although fome bee called Coppy-holders, fome Cuftomary, fome Tenants by the Virg, fome bafe Tenants, fome bound Tenants, and fome by one name, and fome by another; yet doe they all agree in fubftance and kinde of Tenure, though differ in fome ceremonies and kinde of ferving, and therefore the name is not the matter, but the Tenure.

Hee fhall bee faid a perfon fufficient to be a Coppy-holder, who is of himfelfe able, or by another to doe the fervice of a *Coppy-holder*; as an infant may bee a Coppy-holder for his Gardein, and prochein

Infant Itin Covert *Lunatick Nemy* 13. *Eliz.Dier.*301

H 2   any

any may doe the service ; so may a feme
Covert, and her husband shall doe the service : But a lunaticke, or Ideot cannot bee
a Coppy-holder, because they cannot doe
the service themselves, nor depute any other :
and the Lord shall retaine the Coppy-hold of
an Ideot, and not the Queene

A Bond-man or aliene borne may bee a
Coppy-holder, and the King or Lord cannot
seise the same.

But a man cannot be a *Coppy-holder* unto
a Mannour, whereof hee himselfe is Lord,
although hee bee but *Dominus pro termine
annorum*, or *in Iure Vxoris*.

WHAT

WHAT SHALL BE SAID
such Lands, or other things as are demisable by *Coppy*, and may be
holden by Coppy.

IT may bee said of *Coppy-hold* Lands, as is
afore-said of the Tenants ; they may differ in name, but not in nature : As some called *Coppy-hold* Lands, some customary
Lands, some bound Lands, some base Lands,
some ancient Lands, some demeasne Lands,
some encrease Lands, some Mollendes,
some waste Lands, some worke Lands,
some loose Lands, and some Vierge-
lands.

And although *coppy-hold* lands bee spe-
cially so called, because it is holden by Coppy of Court Role, customarie lands because of some speciall custome ; Bond lands
because of the Bond, Tenure, base lands because of Base Tenure, ancient lands, be-

cause

caufe of the old demife , demeafne Lands
becaufe of its new demife , and late being in
the hands of the Lord of the Mannour; increa-
fed lands, becaufe it is late purchafed, and laid
to the Mannour : Mollands, becaufe it is holden by eafie rents , or no rents at all ; wafte
land, becaufe it hath beene lately improved
out of the wafte of the Mannour ; Worke
lands, fuch as hath common appendant belonging to it ; lofe land , becaufe it is holden by uncertainty of Rents; and Veirge
land, becaufe it is holden by the Veirge :
Yet al the faid lands are holden in one general
kinde, that is, by cuftome, and continuance
of Time , and the diverfity of their names
doth not alter the nature of their Tenure.

It feemeth by *Littleton*, that onely Lands
and Tenements are demifable by Coppy:
And therefore if the Lord of a Mannour
will grant the rent charge, or the office of
Stewardfhip, or Baylewicke of his Mannour
by Coppy, or a common in groffe by Coppy,
thefe bee not good grants, becaufe they
lye not in Tenure, and alfo becaufe the *Cuftome* doth not extend unto them, but
common appendent to a Tenement or Coppy-hold lands may be demifed with the Tenement by Coppy.

Demeafne lands which within time of memory,

mory have beene occupied by the Lord himſelfe, or his Farmour, is not good to be granted by Coppy, becauſe of the newneſſe of the grant, yet by continuance of time it may be good Coppy-hold, when the memory of the contrary is worne away, as hath beene ſaid before. Neither can the Lord that granted ſuch a Coppy, put out his *Coppy-holder* during his life that granted the ſame, becauſe hee ſhould not bee received to diſable his owne grant. If a Coppy-holder doe Surrender his coppy-hold into the Lords hands, meerely to the uſe of the Lord, I doubt whether the Lord may grant this againe by Coppy, as hee may where it cemes unto him by forfeiture, or by eſcheat, becauſe it is made percell in demeaſne by his owne acceptance, and not by the Act of the Law, *quære.*

Note that neither the Statute of *Weſt.* 2. *de donis conditionalibus*, nor any other Statute, that hath not Coppyholds named in it, doth extend to Coppy-hold Lands, as the Statute *Staple.* 27. *Ed.* 3. nor the Statute of Hereſie 2. *Hen.* 5. nor the Statute of Wills 32. *Henry* the eight, nor the Statute of *Limitation*, made the ſame yeere as is now

now taken *contra* to Master *Brooke in novel cases*. 426.

But though a gift in Taile of a Coppy-holder, be not contained in the same Statute of *West*. the second : Yet I thinke in such Mannour, where time out of minde they have used to make gifts in Taile of Coppy-hold *Lands*, there such gifts bee good at this day, and they may make protestation in the nature of any Writ, as appeareth by *Little-ton*.

WHAT SHALL BE SAID
a good Surrender.

AS in the conveying of Free Lands there is required some ceremony and publicke notice, so is there in the assuring of Coppy-holds necessarily some publicke Fact to bee done therein, which is the Surren-der

der. In which ceremony, there is contained two effects, the one what is surrendered and to whose use; the other, that it bee done with the Lords good will, and for that cause, it is surrendred into his hands. And although there bee divers wayes of Surrender in severall Mannours, as within some Mannhours to surrender by the hand of another Coppy-holder, and in some other to surrender to the Stewards hands, in some to the Bayliffes hands, and some by giving a yard to the Steward, in some by giving his hand, or his glove, which bee outward signes of his intent: Yet in all those kindes the words of Surrender must not bee divers, but one, and to one effect; and, must be either words of Surrender expressed, or words of Surrender implyed; and therefore if a Coppy-holder will bargaine and sell his Land to *I. S.* and this is found by the Homage, and *I. S.* prayeth to bee admitted Tenant, yet the heire of the Coppy-holder shall avoyde the Admission, because of the insufficiency of the Surrender, taking by the words of Bargaine and Sale, and not by words of Surrender, *epi. Sigr. Dier 8. Dier Eliz. Lou ill dit. que relees ne vault inure Come une surrender.*

If a Coppy-holder commeth into the

I   *Court*

If a Coppy-holder will in the presence of other Coppy-holders of the same Mannour, say that hee is content to Surrender his coppy-hold lands to the use of *I. S.* this is no good Surrender : But if hee saith, hee doth surrender into the hands of the Lord to the use of *I. S.* if the Lord will thereunto agree, this is a good Surrender, whether the Lord will or not.

If the Tenant will Resigne his Interest in the Court, into the Lords hands, therewithall for the Lord to doe his will, this is a good Surrender if it bee accepted.

If a *Coppy-holder* will say hee will bee no longer the Lords Tenant, though these words bee recorded, yet this is no good Surrender.

If a Coppy-holder for life take a new Estate

Estate for life by coppy, this is a surrender of his first estate.

But if a coppy-holder for life will take a Lease of the same by Indenture for life, this is not a good Surrender of the Coppy-hold: *Quare.*

If a Coppy-holder commeth to the Lord, and telleth him, that for the preferment of his Sonne in marriage, with such a mans daughter; his will is, to give his Land presently to his Sonne, and desireth the Lord that he would be contented therewith, this is no good Surrender.

But if he had said these words in the Lords *Court*, and the same recorded, or found by Homage as a Surrender, and so presented, then this had beene a good Surrender without any other words of Surrender.

THAT

THAT A COPPY-HOLDER

must bee admitted Tenant, and *what shall be said a good admittance of a COPPY-HOLDER.*

By Sergeant *Walmesley* 12. *Eliz.* 291. 292.

IF a Coppy-hold descend unto a married woman, and her Husband take the profits thereof, and suffer a Court day to passe without admittance of his Wife, and then the Wife dyes, the Husband shall not be Tenant by the curtesie, but in the 12. *Eliz. Dyer* 291. 292. it seemeth that the contrary should bee the better opinion.

30. *Hen.* 8. *Dier.* 42. 16. there.

An entry before admittance is no forfeiture, without an especiall custome pleaded, but the heire may make a forfeiture for *non* payment of the Rent, as the custome was there pleaded before admittance.

If a Coppy-hold be surrendred unto the use of a stranger upon condition, and the condition

condition be broken, the party that made the Surrender may reenter and bee a Coppyholder to all intents, without any new admiſſion, for he did depart with the Land but upon a condition.

Alſo if a Surrender of a Coppy-hold bee made to the uſe of a ſtranger for Life, and the Lord makes a grant thereof, to the ſame ſtranger in Fee, this ſhall not binde the heire of the Tenant, but that hee may enter after the death of the grantee; for hee tooke the Land by the Surrender, and not by the grant made by the Lord : for the Lord is but an inſtrument for the conveyance of the Land; for if I make a Surrender unto the Lord *ea Intentione*, that hee ſhall grant over unto ſuch a man, if the Lord will not grant the ſame, I may then re-enter, but the ſtranger hath no meanes to enforce the Lord to grant the ſame over unto him, but hee may maintaine Treſpaſſe againſt the Lord, if hee doth ſuffer me to re-enter, and this is the opinion at this day.

The Lord of a Mannour hath that prerogative in his Coppy-holds, that no ſtranger can bee his Tenant thereof, without his ſpeciall aſſent, and admiſſion, and for that

cauſe

cause a Coppy-hold shall not bee lyable to any executions of Statutes, or recognizances, neither shall be *Assets*, in debt or *Formidon*, neither is contained in any the Statutes afore-named, for if it were, then should the Lord be forced to have a Coppy-holder whether hee would or no, which is against the nature of a coppy-hold.

And therefore a stranger can never enter, though a Surrender made to his use bee accepted, except hee bee admitted Tenant, but otherwise of the heire, for hee may enter and take the profits before the Admittance after the death of his Father.

Admittance may be three manner of waies, an expresse admission, by the words entred into the Court Role, *viz. Vnde admissus est Tenens*, or by acceptance, or implication, as if the Lord wil accept the rent by the hands of a stranger: thirdly, by admitting one Coppy-holder, in some cases the Lord shall admit another by implication to some purposes, and to these three may bee added a fourth, which is by the entry of the Sonne, after the death of his Father, and the

Tenant

Tenant in Dower after the death of her
Husband, which is lawfull without admiffion, till the next Court, and then they muft
pray to be admitted, &c.

If a Coppy-holder doe furrender his
Land to the ufe of *I. S.* and the Lord doth
grant the fame to *I. S.* accordingly, and
thereupon hee enters, yet hee is no good
Coppy-holder, till hee bee admitted : But
if *I. S.* appeareth at the Lords Court, and
paffeth on the Lords homage, or the Lord
accepts his Rent or his Fine for the fame
Coppy.hold, now hee is become a good
Coppy-holder without any further Admiffion.

If a Coppy-holder furrendreth his Land
to the ufe of *I. S.* for life, the Remainder to
the ufe of *R. N.* for life, and the Lord granteth
the fame accordingly, and admitteth *I. S.* it
feemeth this is a good admiffion to *R. N.* that
is in the Remainder.

A *Coppy-holder* in Fee dyeth feifed, his
heire may make a furrender to the ufe of
a ftranger, without admiffion : *quære.* But
if a *Coppy-holder* furrender to the ufe of *I. S.*
this *I. S.* cannot furrender to the ufe of a
ftranger,

In Trefpas by *Higge* againft *Felfton.*

ſtranger, without being firſt admitted himſelfe.

    Ifa Coppy-holder Surrender all uſe of two
joyntly , and they are admitted , if the one
of them dyeth , the ſurviver needeth not to
bee admitted againe for the moytie : But
if a Coppy-holder having Iſſue two daughters, and they are admitted , and then the
one of them dyeth , the other muſt needs bee
admitted for the other moyty , for ſhe takes
the ſame by diſcent.

    L' heire dun Coppy-holder poit prender les pro-
fits avera accion de Treſpas et ſerra poſſeſſio fra-
tris dune Coppy-hold, devant aſcune admittance
12. Eliz. Sigr. Dier 291. poit faire leaſes per
ans. Denby et Bullocks ca.

WHAT

WHAT SHALL BE SAID
a forfeiture of a COP-
PY-HOLD.

THE Tenant by Coppy standeth bound by his Tenure to the Lord, that if hee doth any thing to the Lords dif: inheritance, or in some cases if he doth transgresse the duty of a good Tenant, he shal forfeit his Coppy-holde : But because all offences are not equall, so likewise there are degrees of punishment ; for there is a difference betweene offences done wittingly and willingly, and faults ignorantly and unwillingly committed.

And therefore some offences are forfeitures *ipso facto*, some are onely forfeitures when they are presented and not before, and some are onely fineable.

Forfeitures *ipso facto* are offences that lye in miss-fesans, and bee apparent forfeitures ;

K   that

Forfeitures that lie in *Nonfesans*, are where the offence is not apparent, nor affirmatively to bee proved without prefentment.

Offences Fineable', are offences of contempt, and not of dif-inheritance.

As if a Coppy-holder will in the prefence, and fitting of the Court Baron, fay that the Lord doth extort and exact in due Rents and Services of his Tenants, or fuch other unreverend words, this is onely Fineable,

But if hee will then and there fay, being called forth to bee fworne of his homage, that hee is none of his Lords Tenant, this makes a Forfeiture of his Coppy-hold.

But if hee will there fay, that hee will fhortly devife a way that hee will bee no longer any of the Lords Coppy-holders, this is neither caufe of Forfeiture, nor Fine.

If a Coppy-holder *Sendente curia*, doe ftrike another Coppy-holder, or any other
ftranger

ftranger, this is onely Fineable, and maketh no Forfeiture.

If the Steward sheweth forth a Court Role to proove that *I. S.* is a Coppy-holder and this notwitstanding hee will in the Court fay, that hee is a Free holder and sheweth forth a Free deed, and claime thereby, and teareth in peeces the Court Role, and publisheth the free deed, this is a caufe of Fine and Forfeiture.

But if the faid Tenant will there upon fome colourable doubt, and queftion which may arife, whether hee bee a Free holder, or a Coppy-holder fay to the Steward, becaufe hee knowes not whether the Rent that hee fhould pay, be Free rent, or Coppy-hold rent; hee will pay it with proteftation that the rent may be recorded as it fhall fall out, and with like proteftation offer and do his fervice, though in truth hee bee a Coppy-holder, yet this deferveth neither Fine or Forfeyture.

If a *Coppy-holder* cannot pay his rent, and will not doe his fervice, this offence is on the Negative, and maketh no forfeiture till it bee prefented.

Tenant

Tenant per Copple ne poet facere waſt ne couper bois per vender, mes pro reperacon tantum 9. Hen 4. 12. 43. Ed. 3. 32. 80.

But if a *Coppy-holder* doth Alien his Land by Free deed, or will commit waſte, or demiſe his Coppy-hold contrary to the 'Cuſtome, or will ſue a replevin againſt the Lord, for a Diſtr. lawfully taken for his Rent or ſervice due, or diſclaime in the Land being ſummoned to the Lords Court, or will there claime it as his free hold, or will in any other Court untitle any other Lord unto it, or bee attainted of treaſon or felony, or continue out-lawd, or excommunicate, during the Lords Court, or refuſeth to goe with his Lord or other commiſſioners for that purpoſe in the ſervice of the Prince, to ſuppres Rebells, riots, or unlawfull aſſemblies. All theſe offences bee apparent miſ-feſance and forfeiture *ipſo faſto* without any preſentment.

But if a Coppy-holder being of the grand Inqueſt at the Aſſizes or Seſſions, ſhall indite his Lord of any manner of offence committed againſt the Prince or Lawes of this Realme, or ſhall upon proces Compulſary give evidence againſt his Lord, which is true

in any caufe betweene his Lord and another
Common perfon, or betweene the prince and
his Lord without compulfary proces, or fhall
make any bodily areft of his Lord by the
commandment of the Shriefe or other lawfull
authority, or fhall bring any Action or Suit
againft his Lord in any of the Queenes Courts
(except a Replevin cafe aforefaid) All
thefe laft recited, be caufe of neither
Fines or Forfeitures of any Coppy-
hold.

Alfo a Coppy-holder not claiming his
Coppy-hold after the death of his Ance-
ftor within a yeere and a day, at the
Court, if any bee, it is a forfeiture for
*ever per. opin Catline, Stowells Cafe 372. et
c il penc ceo dee bone cuftome in plufors Mannours.*

If Coppyholders being on a Jury will
not finde the wafte committed, or will not
prefent things prefentable, this is a forfeiture
of their Tenures, if they be Coppy-holders,
by the opinion of *Catlin, Dier,* and *Brooke.* 4.
Eliz. Dier. 211. *pe.* 31. 6. *et* 7. *Eliz.* 233. *b.*
9. *Hen.* 6. 44. *b.*

If a Coppy-holder will not bee fworne to

prefent

preſent ſuch offences as are forfeitures , this
is a forfeiture of his eſtate; ſo if he alien, or
make Coppy-hold free, for tenne pound, the
Lord may enter, for they are wilfull acts,
for which the Lord may enter without preſentment, but for negligent offences, as for
not doing of ſervices , or not acceptance
of a Coppy-hold after the death of his an-
ceſtor, the Lord cannot ſeiſe without preſentment of the homage. And if an Infant
within the yeere after the death of his An-
ceſtor, will not after the Court holden & pro-
clamation made, pray to bee admitted, it is
no forfeiture, unleſſe the cuſtome of the
Mannour be, that an Infant ought to forfeit
his eſtate by ſuch negligence, for it is but a
claime at common-Law, which barres not an
infant, which hath not diſcretion. Betweene
Hautrey and *Buckſhire* and one of his coppy-
holders. 12. *Eliz. Rot.* 96.

If thirteene coppy-holders bee ſworne
in a baſe Court, and twelve agree to give
Verdict, the thirteenth will not, it is not a
forfeiture, for it is a good verdict without
his aſſent, and perhaps it is not agreeing
to his conſcience, and therefore it is
not properly a not doing, or denyall to dœ
his duty.

Quære

Quære, If there be 12. and 11. agree, and
the twelfth will not, for it is not a full Jury.
Pasche. 20. *Eliz. Co. Bank. ve.* 3. *Ed.* 3.
Verdict 10. *ou.* 11. 29. *Ed.* 3. *ibid.* 45.
12. *Hen.* 4. 10. *Sherie.*

WHAT OFFICE OR POWER
entirely, or dividedly the Lord,
Steward, *Free-holders, Cap-*
py-holders, and the Bayliffs
have in the Court Baron.

ALthough the Lord, the Steward, the
Free-holders, the Coppy-holders, and
the Bayliffes of every Mannour, have an in-
termixt and joynt office, and authority in
some cases, and to some purposes : yet to o-
ther purposes their office is distinct and divided, and every of them doth occupy severall places, persons, and parts.

The

The Lord is chiefe to command and appoynt the Steward, to direct and record the Free holder to affere and judge the Coppy-holders to enforme and prefent, Bayliffe to attend and execute, &c.

And all thefe together make a perfect execution of Juftice and Judgements in a Court Baron, and without all thefe a Court Baron cannot be holden in his proper nature, in refpect of all caufes belonging to the perfect jurifdiction of a Court Baron.

And yet a Court Baron may be held by ufe and cuftome, for fome Coppy-hold caufes; though it want one of the fayd parties (viz.) the Free holders, and there in Coppy-hold cafes the Steward doth fupply the place of a Judge: But no other of the parts aforefaid, except the Free holders, can be miffed, or fpared in a Court Baron.

But to make fome more particular demonftration of their diftinct authorities and offices; and firft the Lord as hee is chiefe in place, fo is hee in Authority, and occupieth three feverall Roomes; the one of a Chancelour in cafes of equity, the other of a Juftice in a matter of right, the third of himfelfe in cafes
proper

proper and particular to himselfe.

The Steward doth occupy the parts of severall persons, that is to say, Judge and order in cases of Coppy-hold ; and also a Minister, and Register to enter things into the Court Roles, and in both these to bee indifferent betweene the Lord and his Tenants.

The Free-holders doe likewise fulfill two parts, that is, to affeere, & judge amercements, and also to returne and certifie judgements.

The Coppy-holders also doe hold two severall roomes, *viz.* to enforme offences committed against the Lord within that Mannour, and to present such things as shall be given in charge by the Steward.

The Bayliffe doth also occupie two parts, that is to say, to execute the proces and Commandments of the Court, and also to returne into the Court the Execution of the same proces.

6. *Ed.6. Brook. No.*case.*34.plin.387.* the under-steward in *Court*, without authority of the L. or of the *high-steward*, may demise *Copy-hold*

L   and

& it is a good grant, for it is in full Court; but contrary it is if it be out of Court. *Quare*, if the high steward without authority may demise out of Court.

Finis Lecturæ Calthrop.

A Coppy-holder being indebted, doth *surrender* to his creditor, upon trust that he shall have the Land to satisfie himselfe of the debt, and then to bee *surrendred* backe a-gaine unto him; And after the debt levied, the creditor will not *surrender*, whereby according to the custome of the Mannour, the Tenant pursues an English Bill to the Lord in his Court, by which the trust is prooved by de-position; the Lord seiseth the Land to the use of the first *Coppy-holder* untill &c. And *Wray* was of opinion, that hee may well so doe, for he hath no other remedy, for the Lord cannot imprison him, as the Lord *Chancelour* of England may doe; and that the custome of deposition is good, though some doe doubt: but *Gawdy* agrees, but hee saith that the Lord cannot retaine and keepe the Land, and if hee should so doe, the other shall have a *Subpena*; whereunto *Wray* a-greeth, that hee cannot retaine the Land, but

but feife it and grant it over, which without
feifing hee cannot doe, 25. *Eliz. B.* upon the motion of *Cooke*, who fayd that 14.
Hen. 4. 39. and *Fitz. B.* 18. are according
to their opinions : For a *Coppy-holder* fhall not
have a *Writ* of *Error*, nor falfe judgement,
upon a judgement againft him in *Court* of the
Lord ; but he fhall fue by bill, and thereupon the Lord fhall refeife the Land, upon falfe
judgement given by the *Steward*, and fhall
make reftitution.

If one recover a debt by plaint in *Court
Baron*, thofe of the *Court* have not power
to make execution to the Plaintiffe of the
defendants goods ; but they may diftraine
the defendant, and after the judgement retaine the diftres in their hands in fafegard,
untill the Defendant hath fatisfied the Plaintiffe of that wherein hee is condemned by
the Court, 46. *Hen.* 6. 17. See the Booke
of *Entrees* Fol. 116. 7. *Hen.* 4. 27. In re-
pleyin the defendant faid, that one *Edward
Befdll* brought a writ of *Droit* clofe againft
the Plaintiffe, and one other in the Lords
Court in ancient demeafne, and declared in
nature of Affize, and it was found againft
the plaintiffe, and damages were taxed;
whereby the defendant being then under-Bay-

L 2   liffe,

liffe, by the Stewards commandement, takes the beasts for execution of the damages, and takes and sells them, and delivers the monies to the plaintiffe in Assize ; this is a good plea, and yet this is but a Court Baron. And Fol. 29. by *Hull* ; A man recovers ancient Demeasne-Lands, and damages in a Court of ancient Demeasne, and the Bayliffe may take the beasts of him against whom the recovery is, &c. for execution of Damages in every parcell of the Land holden of the Mannour, although that Land be Frank-fee, and it is not denyed 22. *Assise.* 72. agrees with 4. *Hen.*6. *Mr. Kitch.* 115. where it is used to make execution by *levari facias*, that is a good Custome. 38. *Ed.*3. Custome 133. upon a recovery in Court Baron, the Defendants Cattle were delivered in execution.

WHERE

WHERE A TENANT BY

Coppy may plead a speciall Custome, which is onely proper to him and his predecessors before him.

Ninth *Eliz. Taverner* was sued by the *Lord Cromwel*, for that he had committed waste upon his *Copy-hold*; hee pleads by the advice of *Manwood*, that he and those who before him had the house wherein he dwelt, had such a Custome by *Prescription*, that they might fell Timber-trees, &c. And many arguments were against that Custome, in as much as other Tenants of that Mannour had not such a *Custome*, but were punishable, and had forfeited their Lands for such waste; also that Custome was against common right, and not reasonable; and after long deliberation of the Judges, it was adjudged, that a Tenant may plead a particular *Custome*, as if one prescribe to have a way in the Lords Land, &c. And 19 of *Eliz.* one prescribed that he and those of that Tenement his predecessors, had used to have *Common* of estovers in another Mannour, notwithstanding that the other *Tenants* have not such a *Custome*, and it was good by the advice of all the Justices.

WHERE

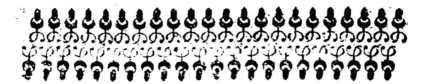

WHERE THE TENANT

may cut downe Trees, destroy
houses by custome, and such
like customes, &c.

FOurth *Ed.* 6. Justice *Dalisons* Reports,
Sanders, and divers Justices; Tenant by
Coppy of *Court* Role may prescribe to have
Wood growing upon the Land. *Montague*,
there is such a custome, and so used in the
Counties of *Mid.* Northland, and other places. *Browne*, it hath beene heere agreed
of late, that Tenant by the Custome may
prescribe to suffer their houses to fall, and
to destroy their houses; so also heere, whereby this is a good Custome. *Montague,*
I have heard a Fable, that a Tenant
by the Custome may digge in the one
part of his house, and burne the other part,
by the Custome : But if you will agree that
the Tenant by Custome shall have the Land
against the Lords Will, to him and his heires
by the Custome ; why then may they not
by the Custome cut downe Wood? *Sanders,*

I

I agree to none of your cafes. *Montague*, furely in the *Chancery* it will bee over-ruled againft you without doubt, and it is neceffary that an Act of Parliament bee made upon it.

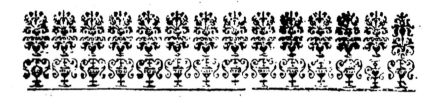

WHERE AND HOW
Tenant by *Coppy*, may make a *Ioynture* to his wife of the fame Land.

A Stranger brings a writ of right againft the husband and wife, in the fame Court where the Land is by plea, and the husband and wife doe appeare, and the demandant doth Count againft them ; and the husband and wife doe defend, and fay that they have more right than the demander, and offer to try it by Battell ; and the demander and Tenants doe Imparle, at which day the demander appeares, and the husband and wife make default, whereby finall judgement is given againft them ; and at the fame Court the

(80)

the Recoverer *Surrenders* the same Land into the Lords hands, to the use of the Husband and Wife, and the heires of their two bodies begotten; and it was sayd, that this assurance hath beene used 1. *Ed.* 6. *Dalisons* reports.

In Monsieur *Wies* reports whether a recovery in Court Baron may defeat an entayle. B. *Regis* 2. *Coment.* 21.

Pellet Hikden : Trin. 36. *Eliz. Rot.* 547. in the Kings bench : Tenant in Tayle, the remainder in Fee; Tenant in Tayle surrenders to the use of *I. S.* in Fee; *I. S.* suffers a Recovery, and vouches the Tenant in Tayle, who vouches the common vouchee, and by speciall Verdict it was found that there was never any recovery before in that manner, and it is not yet adjudged. *Gawdy* and *Clinch*, that the recovery cannot be a Barre; for warranty cannot be annexed to an estate at will; also he shall not recover in value, because of the estate at will. *Fenner* and *Popham* chiefe Justice to the contrary, and that warranty may be annexed to Coppy-hold Land, though it bee an estate at will of the Lord; but as it is an estate in Fee, performing the services and duties, the Law will account them Tenants in Fee : Also recovery in value, being but a fiction in Law, le common vouchee shall bee accounted to have the Land in value of the Coppy-hold, within the

the Mannour ; and the Vouchee, 23.
Henr. 8. Br. Recovery in value 27. that such
a Recovery is uſed in ancient demeaſne upon a writ of right, and Voucher over, and
that of a Free-hold there ; yet enquire of
ſuch a Recovery upon a plaint, there of Land
of Baſe Tenure, for that cannot bee war-
ranted, &c.

But in the Common Bench, in treſpaſſe
brought by *Comb*, againſt *Peares* and *Turner*.
Micb. 36. *et* 37. *Eliz. Rot.* 14. *Bromeley*
Brittain Hall in *Eſſex :* Tenant in ſayle of a
Coppy-hold ſuffers a recovery with Voucher, where no recovery was before; the leſ-
ſer enter, by the Court, that cannot be, but
he ſhall have a Formdone in diſcender ; for
the recovery in Court Baron cannot availe,
becauſe a warranty cannot be annexed to an
eſtate which is at the will of the Lord. Alſo there can bee no Recovery in value ; firſt
becauſe there can be no recovery in value of
Lands out of the Mannour, and the Cop-
py-land is at the Lords will : Secondly, Coppy-hold Land is granted by Coppy only ; and
if by the Recovery the Tenant may have it;
the courſe and *Cuſtome* of the ſeignory would
be deſtroyed, which ſhall not be : Thirdly, the
Lord ſhall looſe his fine, and Fealty alſo ; for

Adjudged in the Common Bench, that a recovery can-not binde an entaile.

M   the

the Coppy is *admiſſus eſt tenens, &c. et Dat.*
Duo de fne pro tali ingreſſu, &c. et fecit
fidelitatem. Fourth *et fiſt, Ph. et Mar.* A
Coppy holder Surrenders to the uſe of his wife
for Life, the remainder to the right heires
of the husband and Wife ; the Wife dyes,
the Husband ſurvives : the queſtion is,
who ſhall hold the Land ; and it was
ſaid, that if the Husband had
no Iſſue by that Wife, then
his heire ſhall have it.

CERTAINE

CERTAINE COPPY-HOLD
cases reported in a certaine BOOKE.

BUt it was said there, that if the Wife had Issue by another Husband, it was there doubted. But it was holden by the better opinion in *Dier*, that the Husband and his heires shall have the Land ; yet if the Husband had first two sonnes, the heires of the Husband, and the heires of the Wife, shall have the Land in common after the deceafe of the Wife, and for proofe thereof hee puts this cafe, if Land bee given for Life, the remaynder to two men and their heires, they cannot have one heire in the cafe : if the Tenant for life dye before them in remainder they shall bee Joine-Tenants, and the heire of the furviver shall have all.: But if none in remainder bee in life, when the Tenant for life dyes, then the heires of them in

M 2   the

the remainder fhall hold in common.

Thirty feventh *Henry* the eighth ; A Coppy holder to the intent to make an affurance to his Wife, fuffers another to bring a Writ of right in the Coppy *Court*, and they joyne the Battell, and at the day the Husband and Wife make default, and finall judgement was given ; and after the recoverer furrenders the fame Land into the Lords hands, to the ufe of the Husband and Wife and their heires ; and a good affurance *per Cur*.

A Coppy holder brings an action upon the cafe againft leffee for waft and good.

A *Coppy holder* makes a Leafe at Will to another, who commits Wafte, which is a caufe of Forfeiture ; the Leffor brings an Action upon the cafe againft the Leffee : By *Walfh, Wefton*, and *Dier*, the Lord may enter, and have Trefpaffe againft the Leffors his Tenant, and therefore it is reafon that hee fhall bee recompenced : But the Lord fhall have a fpeciall Writ of Trefpaffe, and not *vi* and *armis*, becaufe the entry was lawfull. 8 et 9. *Eliz. ibid.*

The Lord *Dacres* enters upon his
Cop-

Coppy holder, and leaseth it to a stranger for yeares ; the Lessee enters, and was ejected by the *Coppy-holder*, and hee brings a Writ of *Electione firme* : The *Coppy-holder* pleades that the Lands are demneable *per Custome* ; and so they were at issue : and hee shewed in evidence a *Coppy* made 13. *Hen.* the eighth, by which a Tenant had surrendred the Lands, to have and to hold, &c. whose estate hee had, and by another Tenant rendring the yearely Rents, Customes, and Services ; and also hee produced certaine Witnesses who proved the Land to bee *Coppie* by the space of 69. yeares. The Plaintiffe, to destroy the Title of that evidence, shewed certaine Rentales that they were Free Lands, &c. 9. *et* 10. *Henry* 7. and not *Coppy* ; and also another Rentall to that intent, in 12. *Henry* 6. which prooved that those *Lands* were leased for twenty yeares : *Per Cur.* this evidence doth not disproove the *Coppy-hold*, for it was not within the time of memory ; but if hee had shewed the *Indenture* of Lease made within 50. yeares, or 80. yeares, so that a man might remember it, then it had beene good, although the statute of limitation extends not unto it, by the Justices, such evidence

M 3   as

as prooves it to be within time of memory is good.

Also by them ; if those Lands bee in the hands of the Lord by forfeiture, Escheate, or Surrender, yet the Custome remaineth; for hee may demise them againe, and the Custome shall bee revived ; but by some men, if by Escheat it bee in the Lords hands, the *Custome* is extinct. 8. *et* 9. *Eliz. Ibidem.*

The Lord cannot increase a fine which is certaine.

Addington Lord of *Harlow* in *Essex,* would encrease the Fines of his Coppy-hold Tenants, which were prooved to bee certaine : And it was holden that hee could not increase them, and it shall be a good prescription to say, alwaies ready to pay such a summe and no more. 18. 19. *Eliz.*

4. *Eliz.* It was mooved by *Manwood* Sergeant, if a Coppy-holder in Fee in right of his Wife doe surrender, the Wife being not examined by the Steward, but by some of the Tenants, the *Custome* permitting it, the Husband dyes : Whether the Wife shall sue by plaint in Nature of a *Cui in vita,* or may enter ? And by him shee may enter, because it is no discontinuance, for that it is a

surrender

furrender to the Lord who hath the reverfion ; for if a Tenant in Tayle enfeoffe him in
the reverfion ; it is no difcontinuance ; but
if fhe had been examined, fhee fhould have bin
barred for ever.

And *Dier*, if a Coppy-holder in Tayle
furrender to the Lord to the ufe of a ftranger,
the Iffue may bring a plaint in Nature of a
Formdone in difcender, and purge the difcontinuance, for it is within the ftatute *De
donis Conditionalibus, Lit Fo.* 16. *Com* 233.
15. *Hen.*8. *Br.tit.Tenant per Copie* 24.

And by *Manwood*, no negative prefcription may prevaile againft a ftatute : And
the Common Law is no other but an ancient Nota
ufage throughout all the Realme ; and a
prime Cuftome may encounter with it , but
not with a ftatute.

And by *Dier*, if after the Surrender the
Lord admit the Wife againe, yet fhee
fhall bee in by her Husband in conftruction of
the Law.

Coppy-hold of inheritance difcends unto
two fifters by two venters, none of them
making entry, and before the Court and admiffion

miffion one of them dyes, her heire fhall have their moyty, and not the other fifter, by *L ier* chiefe Juftice in the Chancery.

Alfo if a Coppy-holder in Taile furrender to another in Fee, who is admitted, this is a difcontinuance, and fo the Husband of his Wifes Coppy-hold: And hee faid, that a re-mitter fh ill be of a *Coppy-hold*, as it fhall be of a Freehold and inheritance at the common Law. 13. *et* 14. *Eliz.*

In the *Dutchy* it was in queftion; whether a Coppy-hold may be entailed or not? And by *Wray* chiefe Juftice, and *Manwood* chiefe Baron; the Tayle was not Fee fimple at the Common Law, if it did not appeare by the Cuftome, and that may be prooved by the Court Roles, or by fome other proofe that there is a recovery by plaint of Formedon, or the Lands had defcended accorling to Land in Tayle, as *poffefsio fratris* fhall not bee of it, or that that the Daughter fhall not inherit, before the fonne which is unckle to the fame. *Egerton* was of counfell with this cafe, which was betweene *Sherington* and another. 22. *Eliz.*

Hanchet and *Roffe* concerning land of *Dicet* in Stepping *Hackney*, a Coppy-holder of inheritance

inheritance dies, the Lord grants the wardship of the Land, during the minority of the
heire, to the Wife being fole ; fhee takes a
Husband and dyes : It was demanded whether the husband fhould have it or not? And
it feemed not, but if it had beene a thing in
which he had intereft to his owne ufe, that
he fhould have it, as a Leafe for yeares ; the
executor fhall have it without admittance
of the Lord ; fo the husband fhall have a
Leafe for yeares made to his Wife, without
admiffion.

By all the Juftices. 17. *Eliz.* If a Coppy-
holder in Fee take an eftate in Tayle by
Charter-hold, or take a Leafe for yeares
by Indenture, his Coppy-hold is con-
founded.

7. *et* 8. *Eliz.* by *Harpour* and others ; a
Leffee for yeares of a Mannour may make
Coppyes (if the Cuftome be fo) to a man and
his heires *fecundum confuetudinem, &c.* for if
the Coppy-holder in fee dye, his heire is in
by defcent, and ought to be admitted, or elfe
he fhall compell the Lord to admit him, for
it is of neceffity. But in Coppies for life or
yeares it is otherwife, for by the death of the
Tenant, there is not any that can compell the

N   Lord

Lord to make him a new Coppy if he will not, but hee may retaine the Land in his owne hands, and therefore the grants of such Coppyes as are expired, made by a lessee for yeares, are voyd.

26. *ELIZ.*

FIrst, Land Demiseable, by Coppy in the time of *Richard* the second, is perfect Coppy-hold; so if it be demised by *Coppy* 15. or 16 yeares.

Secondly, if the Lord purchase the Coppihold of his Tenant for money, this is clearly a surrender, and an extinguishment of the Coppy, ard it is not demiseable by *Coppy* after: But if the Lord enter for forfeiture, without presentment found, that is demiseable by Coppy againe.

Thirdly, If the Lord bring Trespas against a Coppy-holder, who pleads that it is Freehold,

hold, this is a forfeiture, and the Lord may enter.

Fourthly, the Lord cannot feife, becaufe his *Coppy-holder* was fworne to give evidence againft him, for this is no forfeiture.

Fiftly, if a *Coppy holder* diffeife his Lord of other Land, that is not a forfeiture of the Coppy-hold.

Sixtly, if a Coppy-holder dye without heire, and the Lord enter by efcheat, this is demifeable by Coppy againe; but if the Lord afterwards doe make a feoffment, or fuffer a recovery, and after doe repurchafe it, it is not demifeable; but if the Lord reverfe the Judgement upon recovery by error, attaint, or deceit, and hath reftitution, then it is demifeable by Coppy againe.

A diffeifin doth not extinguifh the Cuftome, nor acts done by the diffeifor.

Seventhly, if a Coppy-holder fuffer a recovery to be prefcript at common Law by collufion, or make a Feoffment, or bargaine and fale, and the Lord enters, and makes a leafe for yeares thereof; this Land is not demifeable by Coppy againe.

Eighthly,

Eighthly, if a Coppyholder furrender his Land; to the intent that a ftranger fhall have the Rent out of it by Coppy ; it is no good Coppy-hold Rent.

Ninthly, if there bee two joynt-tenants in Common of a Manour , and a Coppy-holder furrenders to the ufe of one, this is not Coppy-hold Land.

Tentlhy , if the Husband and Wife bee joynt-coppy-holders of the purchafe of the husband during Coverture, and the Husband is attainted of Felony and dyeth, this is not a Forfeiture of any part of the Coppy-hold; but if the purchafe was made before the co-verture, then it is a forfeiture of the moyty.

Eleventh, if two Coppy-holders ex-change by licence , and after the part of the one is recovered by an elder title , hee may enter into the Land which the other hath in ex-change.

Twelvth, If two Coperceners Coppy-holders make partition, and the one is im-pleaded, and doth lofe by juft title, and the recoverer enters into the Land, fhe can-not enter upon her fifter, becaufe fhee did
not

not pray in aid for the rate. A feme Covert Joynt Coppy-holder with another in Fee may furrender her moyty to the ufe of her Husband, and it is good.

Thirteenth, the Kings Steward without any patent of his office feifeth divers Coppy-holds, and afterwards the Lord Treafurer and thofe of the *Exchequer* doe leafe the fame Land for yeares ; and thereupon it was moved, whether Coppies made by the Steward without patent were good? and the Lord *Dier* thought they were good *Copies*, but in the *Exchequer* the Barons were of another opinion.

Foureteenth, a man feifed of a Mannour, to which Coppy-holders for yeares and others are belonging, hee devifeth by teftament the fame Manour to a certaine perfon for payment of his debts, during which time divers Coppies expire, and the devifees grant new Coppies, and afterwards during the terme, the devifees grant in reverfion, and a particular Tenant furrenders in *Court* to the ufe of the grantee, and after the wife of the devifor recovers in Dower part of the Mannour, and hath execution of thofe *Coppy-holds* affigned by the Sheriffe for her Dower : And it was mooved, whether the Wife fhall

N 3   avoyd

avoide those Coppies made by the devisees?
And *Browne* Justice was of opinion that no;
to which *Weston* agreed, for they said, that
those are ordinary things, and which must bee
done of necessity by force of the Custome,
and not any deede or new charge created by
the devisees, who are but officers to execute
the Custome which of necessity must bee
done, for they cannot bee made by any
others who have the possession of the
Mannour; for it hath beene adjudged,
that such Coppyes and ordinary things, as
presentment to a Church made by a disseisor,
or by a Lessee for Life or Yeares shall stand
good, and shall not bee avoyded by reason
of the necessity : but other charges created
by the Heire after the death of the Husband,
as a Lease for yeares Rent charge in which
ther is no such necessity, the Tenant in
dowre shall discharge them, and although
the Wife shall bee adjudged in by her
Husband, yet she shall not have those things
which chance before assignment of her dower. If a Wardship fall, or an avoydance of a
Church, or a villaine regardant hath purchased, and the heire enters, or presents, these
things the heire shall have, and not the Tenant in Dowre, and it may be that the Wife
will never sue for her dower, or peradven-
ture

ture fhee fhall have other Mannours affigned
her for the fame. And as to the reafon, that
it is not a thing of neceffity to grant Coppyes
in reverfion, yet they were of opinion that
becaufe the *Cuftome* doth allow it, it is *Cuftome ley*, and therefore it may be put in execution : For the *Cuftome* is annexed unto
the Land, and not unto the intereft of the
Lord. But *Wray* faid, that of eftates that
are to *Coppy holders* and their heires according to the Cuftome of the Man-
nour, if fuch a Coppy-holder dye without
heire, the Cuftome is determined. If fuch a
Leffor for life or yeares of the fame Mannour
grant new Coppyes they are not good, and
fo there is a diverfity.

A man cannot devife that his friends fhall
make Coppies or hold Courts, for none
fhall make Coppies but he that is Lord of the
Mannour, and hath an intereft.

The Lord of the Mannour fhall have the
government of the Coppy hold during the
infancy of his Tenant : Executors fhall have
a Leafe for yeares of Coppy hold Land
without any new admittance.

The Husband of a Wife that is Coppy-
holder for yeares, fhall not bee newly admitted after the death of the *Wife*, nor bee
tenant by the courtefie.

Where

Where inheritance of a *Coppy-hold* defcends, the heire may enter without admittance; but it was a doubt whether he fhould have an action of Trefpaffe againft a ftranger before admittance; for before admittance he is not properly Tenant; if fuch an heire will not come to the next *Court*; the Lord may make proces againft him.

A *Coppy-holder* fhall have Trefpaffe againft his Lord, if his Lord out him, paying his Services and cuf.omes.

If erronious judgement bee given againft a *Coppy-holder* in the Lords Court, the Lord in his Court may reverfe it, for it is not amendable in any other place or Court.

If the Leffe of a Coppy-hold commit wafte, and the Lord feifeth for forfeiture; the Coppy-holder fhall not have an action of wafte againft his Leffee, as if Tenant for life make a Leafe for yeares, which Leffee maketh wafte, and the Leffor recovers, the Tenant for Life fhall not have an action of the Cafe, but is without remedy; for it was his folly that hee would not have a collatterall covenant of the Leffee that he fhould doe no wafte.

A Coppy-hold is not forfeit for herefie, by the Stat. of 2. *Hen.*5.

A Coppy-holder is not Ter-tenant, but is Tenant at the Lords will; and 'a Coppy-hold is not bound by the ftatute of Wills nor of

Fines,

Fines, nor of Limitations.

A *Coppy-hold* shall not be extended by a statute, Marchant or Staple.

The Husband and Wife being seised of a Mannor to them and the heires of the Husband, hee grants a Rent charge out of it, and dyes, the *Coppy holder* surrenders, the Wife makes another *Coppy*, and dyes, the grantee shall distraine upon the *Coppy-hold*.

If the Lord of a Mannour hath a great waste, and grants a rent charge out of the same, and the *Coppy holders* have *Common* in the waste, and they put in their *Cattell*, the grantee shall distraine them, if they cannot make prescription.

If a *Coppy-holder* surrender to the use of another, and the Lord will not admit him, nor make a grant unto him, the surrender is voyd.

If there be two Joynt *Coppy-holders*, an the one commits a forfeiture, hee shall forfeit but the Moyty.

Lessee for yeares of a *Coppy-hold* shall have an *ejectione firme*; by *Plowden* and others.

If there be a Lease for yeeres of a Mannour, and one Coppy-holder purchase the reversion in fee, this is a destruction of the Coppy-hold, and the Lessee of the Mannour may put him out, and occupy during his terme. 8. *Eliz.* adjudged.

A Coppy-holder purchaseth the Mannour to him and another in fee, the companion may occupy the Coppy-hold joyntly presently 14. *Eliz.*

Nota

Nota, it was agreed in the common Bench, 21.
Eliz. that the bailiffe of a hundred, or of a base
Court may take goods upon *levari facias*; to
give execution to the Plaintiffe, as well as the
Sheriffe; yet they agreed that divers bookes
are against it. 4. *Hen.* 6. 22.
Two Joynt Copy-holders in Fee make a partition, that is good and no forfeiture, nor aliena-
tion. 12. *Eliz.* agreed in dutchy chamber.

If a Coppy-holder surrender, and then the
Lord doth acknowledge a statute marchant,
and after the Lord grants it by Coppy, the
Coppy-hold is liable, for at the time of the
knowledgement it was annexed to the free
hold; but if a Coppy-holder acknowledge a
statute, that is not liable.

If a man enter with force upon a *Copy-holder*,
he shall not have forceable entry, nor indict-
ment, but the Lord shall have it, and upon
restitution to the Lord the *Coppy-holder* shall
enter.

The Lord grants to a *Coppy-holder* his trees
growing, or that shall bee growing upon the
Land, he may fell trees now growing, and no
forfeiture, by reason of the dispensation, but
hee cannot cut the trees which shall grow in
time to come.

If the disseisor of a *Mannour* make *Coppyes*
for life, and the disseisee enter, he shall defeat
them, but of *Coppy-holds* in fee before disseis-
sin, and a new grant of them upon Surrender
in time of disseisin, it is otherwise *per Plowden.*
Popham in *Case Ramsey vers. Arthurs* 29.
Eliz.

Eliz. A *Coppy-holder* may prescribe to have common in the Lords Land.

If a *Coppy-holder* surrender to the use of another, and the Lord grant it to *cesty que use*, making no mention of the surrender, yet it is good, *per Plowden.*

If there bee a Mannour consisting of demeasnes, Free hold and *Customary* Tenements, if the Lord grant certaine of the *Coppy holds* in Fee, the grantee may keepe *Court*, and do homage, and the *Coppy-holders* by their oaths may make presentments of their Customes, or of the death of any Tenant, and the grantee may make in *Court* a new estate by *Coppy*, as if it should be a perfect Mannour; but the stile shall not be, *Curia Mancrij*, but *Curia halimoti, id. est, Convocatio tenentium*, for when they are assembled, they may enforme the Lord of their Customes and duties. It was otherwise adjudged in the *Com bench. 29. Eliz.* betweene *Dodington* and *Chaffin* for parcell of the Mannour of *M.*

It was adjudged in the common Bench 29. *Eliz.* that where Sir *Peter Carew* being solely seised of the mannour of *M.* In the County of *Devonshire* for Life; granted a Coppie in reversion according to the Custome of the Mannour, and dyed before the particular Coppy-holder; this is a good Coppy in reversion against the Lord, in whose hands soever the *Signory should come.*

FINIS.

Errata.

FOl. 4. line 8. for preferment, read preferred; l. 19. for
and read Ayde ; & in the beginning of the l. for is read
and. Fol. 6. l. 23. for compelled, read expell'd. f. 2 6. for
transgression re. trespasse, f. 7. l. 17. for Brad. re. Brook. f. 8
l. 6. re. shall be accompted as able to be. l. 16 for Coppyholders re. Coppyhold. l. 19. for divisable, re. demisable, l. 27,
for Tenements re. Tenants. f. 9. l. 2. for Tenements re. Tenants. l. 23. leave out (it) f. 15. l. 19. for offer re. affeere.
f. 17. l. 9. re. a particular right, f. 18 l. 9. for M. 1. re. West m. 1.
f. 20. l. 9. for eiusmodi re. talem, last li. for clausa re. causa,
f. 21. l. 4. for accident re. incid nt, f. 23. l. 4. for commonly
is lands, re. commonly is in lands, l. 23. for custome Harri-
ott, re. custome of Harriots, l. 24. for of common Æstovers
re. common of Æstovers, f. 25. l. 4. for deceased, re. disseis-
sed, l. 13. for is uncertaine, re. is so uncertaine, f. 28. l. 7.
for both to discusse, re. both be to discusse. f. 29. l. 3. for
transgresse, re. trespasse in divers places, l. 23. for or services, re. doing services, l. 25. for prescribe, re. to prescribe.

CPSIA information can be obtained at www.ICGtesting.com
Printed in the USA
BVOW07s0956290514

354839BV00010B/292/P